THE USBORNE
COMPLETE BOOK OF
ASTRONOMY
& SPACE

SCHOLASTIC INC.
New York Toronto London Auckland Sydney
Mexico City New Delhi Hong Kong

Acknowledgements

Additional editorial and design by Kirsteen Rogers and Karen Webb

Photo credits:
Stuart Atkinson (78, 79); Luke Dodd (59); ESA (14-15); ESA/PLI (22-23); Calvin J. Hamilton (33); Jerry Lodriguss (4);
NASA (6, 9, 11, 14, 20, 20-21, 24, 24-25, 27, 28, 29, 30, 31, 33, 34, 34-35, 37, 42, 43, 46-47, 50, 51, 52, 53, 81);
NASA/ESA (55); NASA Landsat Pathfinder Humid Tropical Forest Project (22); NOAA (23 – top);
Pekka Parviainen (15); Royal Observatory, Edinburgh (1, 2-3); Rev. Ronald Royer (16-17); Robin Scagell (19); Tom
Van Sant/Geosphere Project, Santa Monica (23 – middle left); Frank Zullo (45).

THE USBORNE
COMPLETE BOOK OF
ASTRONOMY
& SPACE

Lisa Miles and Alastair Smith

Edited by Judy Tatchell

Designed by Laura Fearn, Karen Tomlins and Ruth Russell

Cover design by Stephen Wright

Illustrated by Gary Bines and Peter Bull

Consultants: Stuart Atkinson and Cheryl Power

CONTENTS

THE UNIVERSE

THE UNIVERSE

The universe is the name that we use to describe the collection of all the things that exist in space. The universe is so huge that its size is hard to imagine. It is made of millions of stars and planets, and enormous clouds of gas, separated by gigantic empty spaces.

Light years

Distances in space are huge. They are usually measured in "light years". One light year is the distance that light travels in a year, approximately 9.46 million million km (5.88 million million miles). Light travels at a speed of 300,000km (186,000 miles) per second.

Galaxies

Stars group together in huge collections called galaxies. Galaxies are so big that it can take a ray of light thousands of years to travel across one. Planet Earth is in the Milky Way galaxy. This galaxy is about 100,000 light years across. Distances between galaxies are much greater.

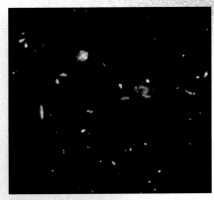

The smudgy little shapes in this photo are some of the most distant galaxies ever seen.

A close-up view of our nearest star, the Sun.

How big?

Nobody knows how big the universe is. It contains millions and millions of galaxies. As astronomers develop new, more powerful telescopes, they discover even more galaxies. So far, astronomers have spotted galaxies that are up to 15,000 million light years away.

Planet Earth

The Earth is one of nine planets that travel around, or orbit, the Sun. Together, the Sun and everything that is in orbit around it are called the Solar System.

The nearest natural object to the Earth is the Moon, which orbits the Earth. It takes a ray of light 1½ seconds to travel from the Moon to the Earth.

When you look at the night sky, you are looking out upon millions and millions of stars.

The Moon in orbit around the Earth.

The path of the Moon's orbit.

Earth

Stars in space

There are millions and millions of stars in every galaxy. A star is a ball of hot gas, which produces heat and light from nuclear reactions within its core. Stars come in lots of sizes and brightnesses.

Nearest stars

The closest star to Earth is the Sun. It is about 150 million km (94 million miles) away. A ray of light takes eight minutes to travel from the Sun to Earth.

The second closest star to Earth is Proxima Centauri. It is about 4¼ light years away – that is, 40 million million km (25 million million miles).

THE STORY OF THE UNIVERSE

The story of how the universe was created is not fully understood. Most scientists believe that it began with a huge explosion. They call this idea the Big Bang theory.

The fireball spreads out and the universe starts to expand.

Big Bang theory

According to the Big Bang theory, the universe was formed in an unimaginably violent explosion, called the Big Bang.

Scientists think that the explosion happened over 15,000 million years ago and that nothing existed before this event. Time itself began with the Big Bang.

After the Big Bang

The Big Bang created a huge fireball, which cooled and formed into tiny particles. Everything in the universe is made up of these tiny particles, called matter. The fireball spread out and the universe began to expand.

A dark universe

Over time, the fireball cooled into thick clouds of gases. The gases then collected into dense clumps. The universe was so dense that light could not travel far within it, so it was very dark.

Thick clouds of gases collect into vast clumps of dense matter.

Galaxies form

The temperature of the universe continued to fall but it was still unimaginably hot. After thousands of years, the temperature fell to a few thousand degrees. The fog cleared and light could travel farther. Galaxies formed from the dense clumps of matter.

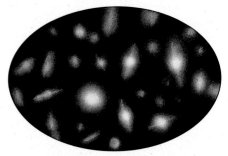

Stars and galaxies begin to form and the universe becomes see-through.

Our Solar System

About 10,000 million years after the Big Bang, the Sun, Earth and the other planets of our Solar System were formed near the edge of the Milky Way galaxy. Even today, parts of the universe are still forming.

Almost 10,000 million years after the Big Bang, the Solar System forms.

Evidence for...

One reason why most scientists think that the Big Bang theory is correct is that a weak signal, like an echo, has been detected from space by powerful radio telescopes. It could be that this echo is from the energy in the early fireball, which spread out into space after the Big Bang.

The energy from the Big Bang explosion spread out into space, creating an echo.

...and against

There is a problem, though. Astronomers have calculated that if the universe contains only the matter that we know about, it would have expanded too quickly after the Big Bang for galaxies to form.

For the Big Bang theory to be true, the universe must contain a lot more matter than we know about. Much more matter needs to be discovered before we can account for all of the "missing matter" that should exist.

We may only know about 10% of the universe. The rest is still to be found.

What will happen to the universe?

Space scientists have several theories about what might happen to the universe in the future. Three of these are described below.

Slowing Down theory

If not much more matter than we know about exists out in space, the universe could go on and on expanding.

In this endlessly expanding universe, everything would simply fade away. Old stars would die and the galaxies would stop making new stars. Eventually the whole universe would become just a mist of cold particles.

The universe could slow down and then simply fade away.

Big Crunch theory

If more matter exists than we know about, a pulling force, called gravity, may eventually slow down the expansion of the universe. It will pull everything back until the galaxies collide. There could then be a Big Crunch, like the Big Bang in reverse.

The galaxies could collide in a Big Crunch.

Oscillating Universe theory

Some scientists think that the universe works like a heart, beating in rhythm. They believe that it expands, then it shrinks, then it expands again, and so on. So a Big Bang is followed by a Big Crunch, in a repeating cycle.

Big Bang   Big Crunch   Big Bang

Space detectives

We don't yet know enough to say for sure how the universe works. Astronomers are like space investigators, using powerful equipment, such as the radio telescope on the right, to unravel the mysteries of the universe.

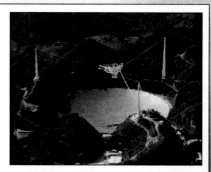

The Arecibo dish in Puerto Rico. This is the largest radio telescope in the world.

FINDING OUT ABOUT SPACE

Here are some examples of the ways in which astronomers find out about the universe, and the techniques and equipment that they use.

Optical telescopes

Telescopes which use light to magnify objects are called optical telescopes. Astronomers use powerful optical telescopes to look deep into space. Many are built high up on mountains, so that they are above much of the Earth's hazy, polluted atmosphere.

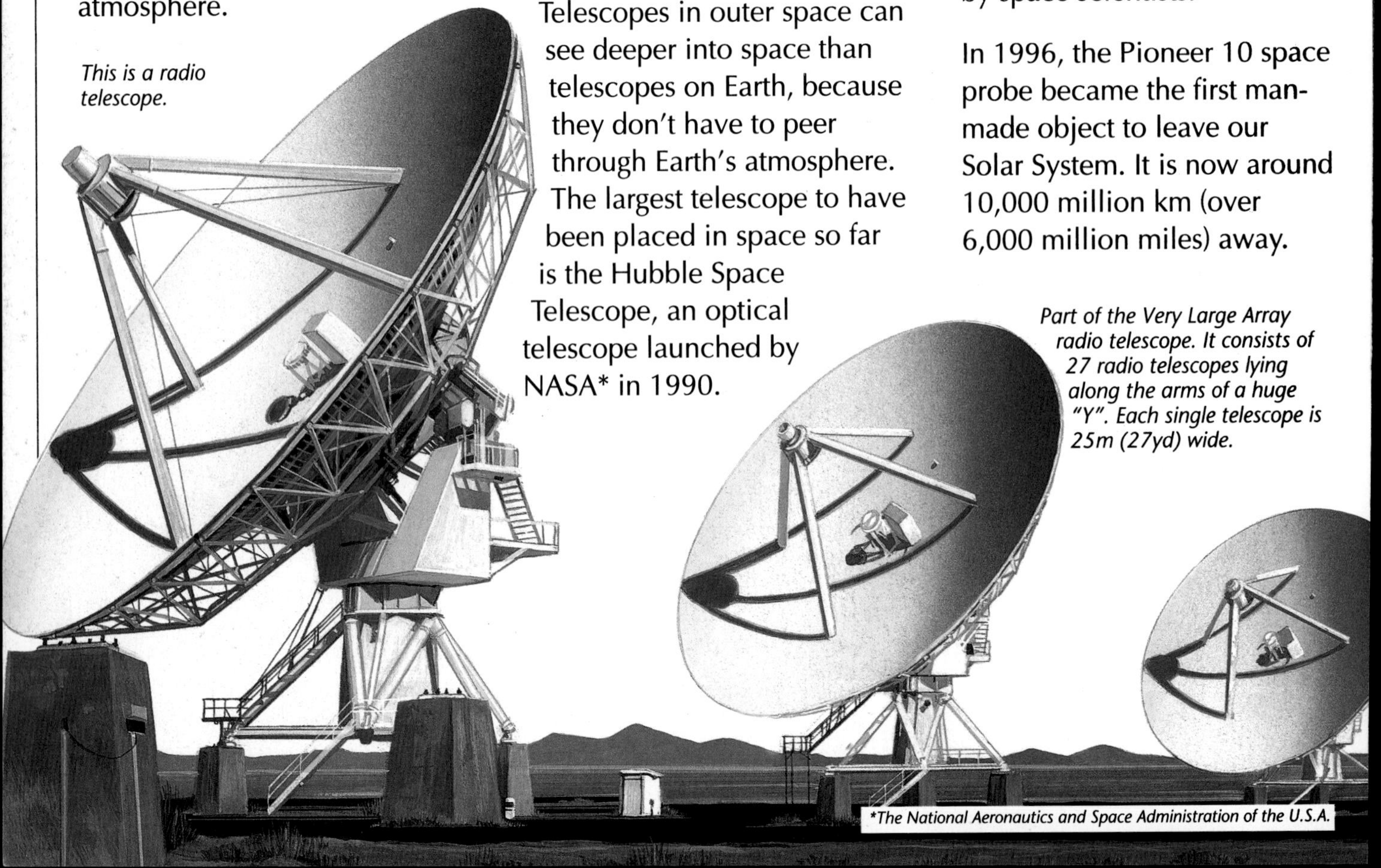

This is a radio telescope.

Radio telescopes

Radio telescopes use very large dishes, or antennas, that collect the faint signals given out by objects in space. They enable astronomers to detect things that are simply too dark or too far away to see, even through the most powerful optical telescope.

The largest radio telescope is the Arecibo dish in Puerto Rico (see page 9). Its 305m (1,000ft) wide dish is built into a natural valley. The picture below shows part of the Very Large Array radio telescope, in New Mexico.

Telescopes in space

Telescopes in outer space can see deeper into space than telescopes on Earth, because they don't have to peer through Earth's atmosphere. The largest telescope to have been placed in space so far is the Hubble Space Telescope, an optical telescope launched by NASA* in 1990.

Space stations

Space stations are bases orbiting the Earth. Scientists and astronauts on board use them to do experiments and to find out how the human body reacts in space. The two largest space stations built so far, Skylab and Mir, have both also been used to observe the stars and planets.

Space probes

Unmanned space probes are sent to investigate deep space and transmit their findings back to Earth. Many carry cameras, which take detailed photographs of distant worlds. They beam the photos back to Earth, where they are studied by space scientists.

In 1996, the Pioneer 10 space probe became the first man-made object to leave our Solar System. It is now around 10,000 million km (over 6,000 million miles) away.

Part of the Very Large Array radio telescope. It consists of 27 radio telescopes lying along the arms of a huge "Y". Each single telescope is 25m (27yd) wide.

*The National Aeronautics and Space Administration of the U.S.A.

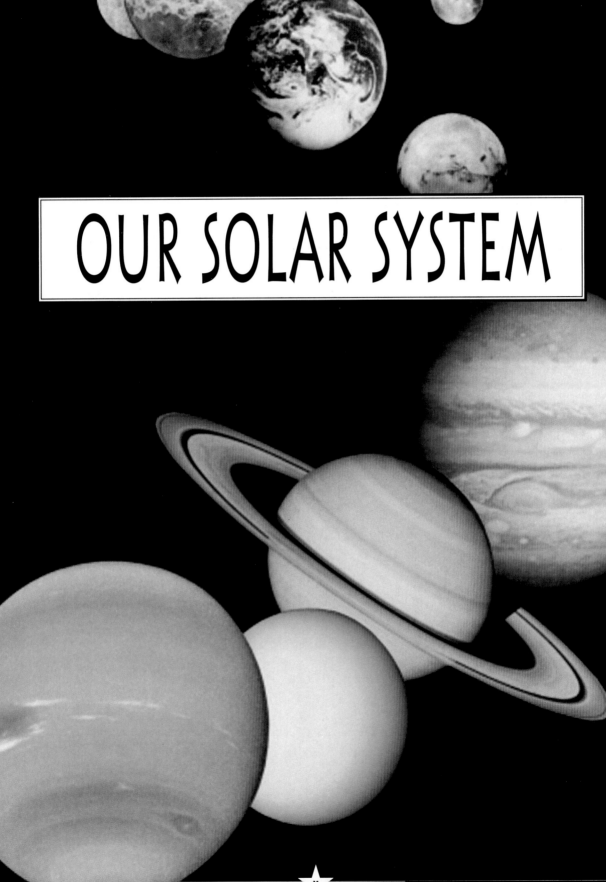

OUR SOLAR SYSTEM

Shown from the top: Mercury, Venus, Earth and Moon, Mars, Jupiter, Saturn, Uranus and Neptune, taken by various space probes.

OUR SOLAR SYSTEM

The Solar System is made up of the Sun and all the objects that spin around it, from planets and moons, to chunks of rock and huge amounts of dust. The word *solar* means "of the Sun".

The Sun

The Sun is a star; that is, a massive ball of exploding gases. It applies a pulling force, called gravity, to everything within a range of around 6,000 million km (3,750 million miles), locking them into orbit around it.

The Sun is bigger than everything else in the Solar System put together.

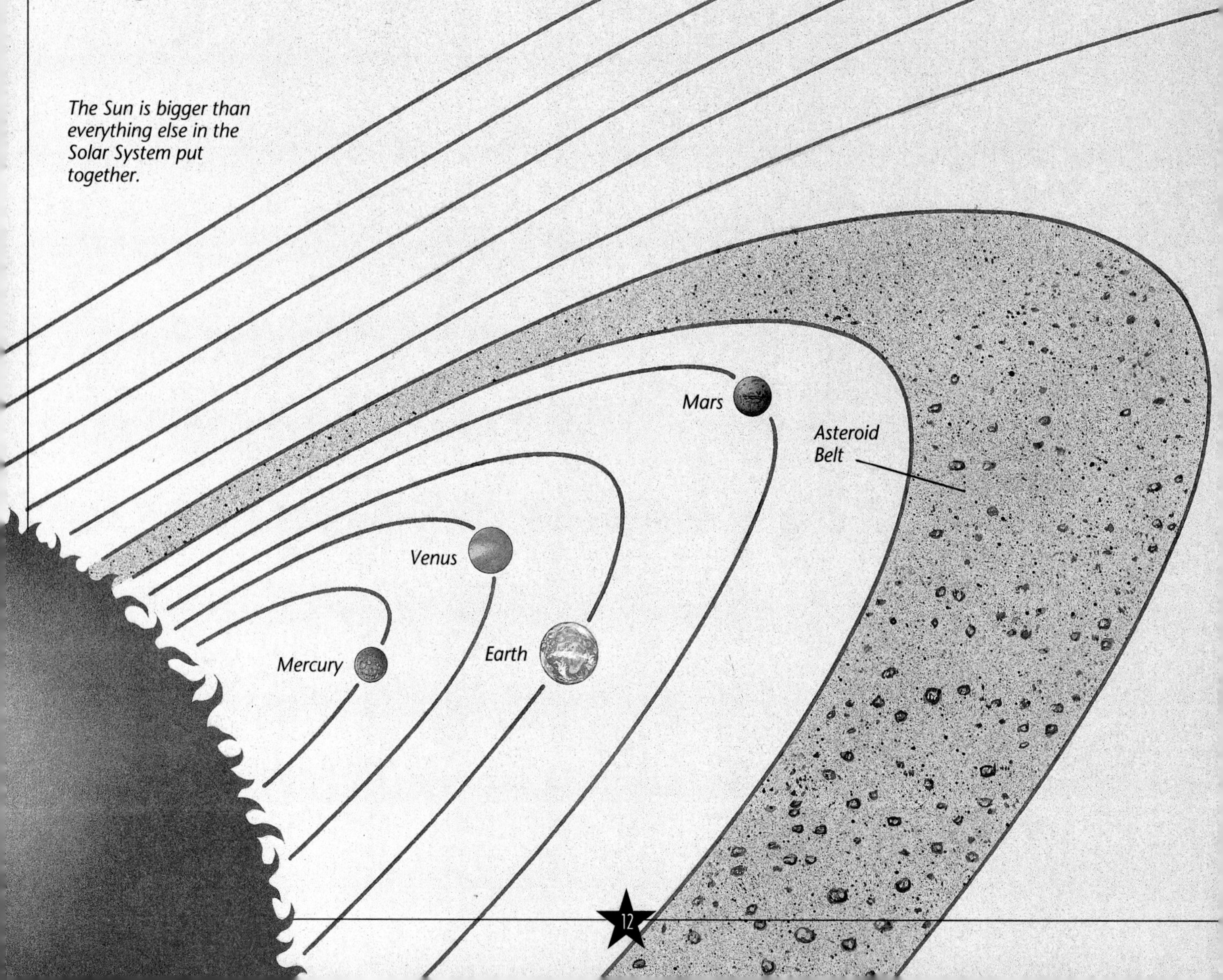

The planets

The largest things that spin around the Sun are the planets. At the moment, scientists know of nine of them, but there may be more that haven't been discovered yet. They travel around the Sun in near-circular paths, called orbits. The four planets closest to the Sun, called the inner planets, are small, rocky and compact. These are Mercury, Venus, Earth and Mars.

This picture shows the planets in orbit around the Sun.

Mars

Asteroid Belt

Venus

Earth

Mercury

The planets farther away from the Sun are called the outer planets. These are Jupiter, Saturn, Uranus, Neptune and Pluto. They are made of ice, gas and liquids, and all except Pluto are larger than the inner planets.

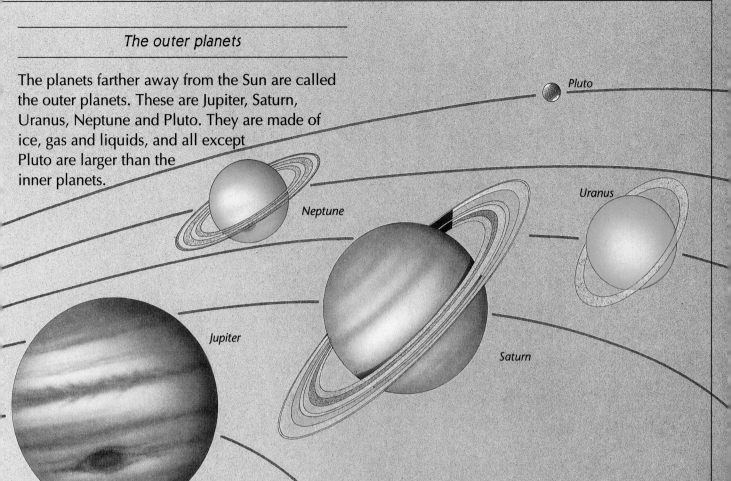

Pluto

Neptune

Uranus

Jupiter

Saturn

Asteroids

Asteroids are large chunks of rock, or rock and metal. They were formed along with the rest of the Solar System around 5,000 million years ago. They orbit the Sun like the planets. Some asteroids have a long, oval-shaped orbit which takes them far away from the Sun. Others travel ahead of or behind the planets, but most lie between Mars and Jupiter in a band called the Asteroid Belt.

Comets

Comets are like huge, dirty icebergs orbiting the Sun. Their paths take them far away, and they only come near the Sun for a short time. They are mostly named after who discovered them. For example, Halley's Comet is named after the astronomer Edmund Halley.

Moons

Many planets have moons in orbit around them, in the same way that our Moon orbits the Earth. Some planets have many moons; for example, Saturn has at least 18.

There are different types of moons. Some are rocky; others contain ice and liquid as well as rock. Many, like our Moon, have craters, mountains and valleys. Some we know little about, because they have not been photographed in much detail.

Meteoroids

Small pieces of debris floating around in the Solar System are called meteoroids.

When they fall into the Earth's atmosphere, they burn up and make a bright streak across the sky. Falling meteoroids are called meteors. Some meteors actually hit the Earth's surface. These are called meteorites.

THE SUN

Like all stars, the Sun is a massive ball of exploding gas. Inside, tiny particles, called atoms, of hydrogen gas join together to form another gas called helium. This joining process is called nuclear fusion and gives off huge amounts of heat and light. This is sunshine. Without it, life could not exist on Earth.

How big?

Sun •   Betelgeuse

The Sun measures about 1.4 million km (about 875,000 miles) across. Inside, it could hold more than a million planets the size of the Earth. But compared with the size of some of the other stars in the universe, the Sun is not all that big. This picture shows the size of the Sun compared with one of the biggest stars – Betelgeuse.

The structure of the Sun

Core. The Sun's core is twenty-seven times the diameter of the Earth. Its temperature is over 15 million °C (27 million °F).

Radiative zone. Heat produced in the core spreads through this part in waves.

Convective zone. This carries the Sun's energy up to the surface. The arrows show its churning motion.

The photosphere is the Sun's surface. It is made of churning gases.

The corona is the outer part of the Sun's atmosphere. It extends for a vast distance, but is very faint and cannot be seen unless the Sun is blocked out, for instance, by the Moon during an eclipse (see pages 16-17).

Sunspots

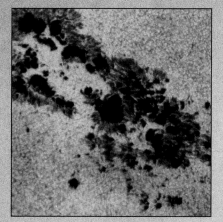

A sunspot, photographed from Earth using special photographic equipment.

The Sun's surface is sometimes marked with small, dark patches, called sunspots. They are areas of the Sun's surface that are slightly cooler than their surroundings. Occasionally, sunspots form in groups that can become enormous. The largest group yet seen covered an area of 18,130 million square km (7,000 million square miles).

Glowing gases

Clouds of glowing gases often surround sunspots, hovering just above the Sun's surface. These are called faculae. Huge loops of gas, called prominences, rise up from the surface at speeds of up to 600km (375 miles) per second. Explosions of radiation (waves of energy produced by the Sun), called solar flares, are even more violent and spectacular.

This photo shows the Sun's endlessly churning surface.

The solar wind

An aurora is an eerily beautiful display of moving light, caused by the solar wind. It is visible from areas in the far north and the far south of the Earth.

The Sun blows a constant stream of invisible particles out into space, in all directions. This is called the solar wind. Solar wind hits the Earth all the time, but you don't feel it, because the Earth's magnetic forces deflect and soak up its energy.

When particles become trapped near the Earth's north and south poles, they create a beautiful light display, called an aurora. In the north, this is called the aurora borealis, or the northern lights. In the south, it is called the aurora australis, or the southern lights.

ECLIPSES

As the Earth and Moon move in space, they sometimes block each other from the Sun's light. This is known as an eclipse. Every now and then you can see an eclipse. It is an exciting event and often makes the news. There are two different types – a lunar eclipse and a solar eclipse.

Lunar eclipses

A lunar eclipse happens when the Earth passes between the Sun and the Moon. The Moon moves into Earth's shadow.

A lunar eclipse can be seen from the side of the Earth that is in darkness. The Moon looks dim in the sky. It often glows a reddish shade.

There is usually one eclipse every year. Eclipses can be seen with the naked eye, but look better through binoculars.

A total lunar eclipse

Like any shadow, the Earth's shadow is lighter at the edges and darker in the middle. If the Moon passes into the darker part, called the umbra, a total eclipse takes place. The Moon looks very dark.

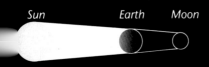

Sun   Earth   Moon

A total lunar eclipse. The Moon is in the Earth's shadow.

A partial lunar eclipse

The Moon passes into the Earth's shadow.

Penumbra

Earth

Umbra

Moon

A partial eclipse happens when part of the Moon stays in the lighter part of the shadow, the penumbra. The Moon turns less dark than during a total eclipse.

A partial eclipse also occurs if the Moon misses the umbra completely and only goes through the penumbra. It is much less noticeable, though.

The big photograph on this page shows a total eclipse of the Sun (a solar eclipse – see opposite). The Sun is blocked out completely by the Moon's shadow. The bright glow of light around the dark shadow is the corona, the outer part of the Sun's atmosphere.

Solar eclipses

A solar eclipse happens when the Moon passes between the Sun and the Earth, blotting out sunlight to part of our planet. Astronomers travel all over the world to see solar eclipses. They only happen about once every three to four years and usually only last for two to three minutes.

During a total solar eclipse, the corona is visible to the naked eye. Usually, astronomers have to use special equipment to see it. You can look at the total eclipse but be very careful not to glimpse the Sun's rays immediately before or after it.

Seeing the eclipse

A solar eclipse can only be seen from the places on Earth which are covered by the Moon's shadow. It only covers a small part of the Earth's surface.

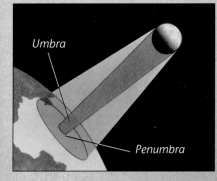

Umbra

Penumbra

The series of pictures on the right shows what happens during an eclipse.

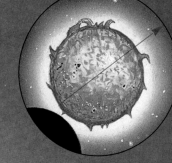

1. The Moon approaches the Sun.

2. The Moon slides over the face of the Sun.

3. The Sun's light is partly blocked out. This is a partial eclipse.

4. In a total eclipse, the Sun is blocked out. Only the corona can be seen.

LOOKING SAFELY
The best way to see a solar eclipse is to project an image of it (see page 15). DO NOT look straight at the eclipse, or view it through smoked glass, or look at it through binoculars or a telescope. The rays from the Sun may blind you.

The diamond ring effect

This is a dazzling effect that sometimes happens during a solar eclipse. Immediately before and after the eclipse, a big ray of sunlight may shine out, which looks like a diamond.

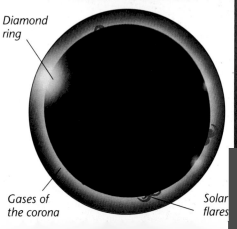

Diamond ring

Gases of the corona

Solar flares

MERCURY

Of all the planets in our Solar System, Mercury is the closest to the Sun. It orbits at a distance from the Sun of about 60 million km (around 37½ million miles).

Since Mercury is the planet nearest the Sun, it orbits the Sun in a shorter time than any other planet.

Mercury

Sun (not shown to scale)

Tiny planet

Compared with most other planets in the Solar System, Mercury is small. Only Pluto is smaller. Mercury's diameter is 4,878km (3,031 miles). The Earth's diameter is nearly three times greater.

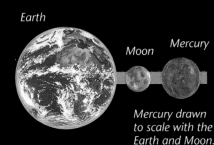

Earth

Moon *Mercury*

Mercury drawn to scale with the Earth and Moon.

Heat and cold

Mercury is so near the Sun that daytime temperatures can reach 427°C (800°F). This is over four times as hot as boiling water.

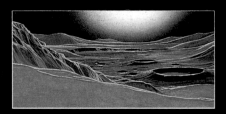

Mercury's desolate, cratered surface.

But at night, the temperature can fall to -183°C (-300°F). Some of the craters on Mercury are so deep that the sunlight never reaches the bottom to warm them up. They stay extremely cold.

Years and days

Mercury's year (the time it takes to orbit the Sun) takes 88 Earth days. So a year on Mercury is less than a quarter of a year on Earth.

Mercury spins slowly. Each day (the time it takes to spin around once) is equal to 59 Earth days. There are fewer than two days in the Mercury year. The long periods facing away from the Sun explain why it gets so cold at night.

Seeing Mercury

You can sometimes see Mercury in the sky just after sunset or just before sunrise. Look for it low in the sky. It will look like a white star, shining steadily.

At its brightest, you can see Mercury with the naked eye, but it is best to view it using a telescope or binoculars.

The bright spot in the middle of this photograph is Mercury.

Mercury's phases

Mercury's brightness and shape appear to change as it goes around the Sun. The changes are called phases. It is possible to see Mercury's different phases, but only through a powerful telescope.

When Mercury is nearer to the other side of the Sun, it looks small and faint because it is so far away. More of it looks lit up, though. (See gibbous and full phases below.)

As it comes around the Sun, Mercury appears bright and relatively large because it is closer to us. Less of its surface looks lit up, though. (See crescent phases below.)

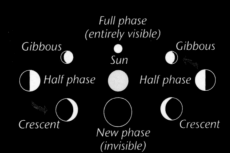

Full phase
(entirely visible)

Gibbous

Gibbous

Sun

Half phase

Half phase

Crescent

Crescent

New phase
(invisible)

Mariner 10, the only space probe to visit Mercury.

Space probe

The only mission to Mercury so far was launched by the U.S.A. in 1973. The unmanned space probe was called Mariner 10.

Mariner 10 mapped the surface of Mercury in detail. The probe discovered that the planet has no atmosphere surrounding it and no water, so nothing could possibly live there. Its barren, rocky surface is covered with sharp-edged craters.

A Mariner 10 photograph of Mercury's surface.

VENUS

This planet is a similar size to the Earth. It orbits the Sun at a distance of about 110 million km (70 million miles). From its mostly flat surface rise several areas that resemble the continents of the Earth.

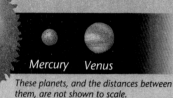

Mercury   Venus

These planets, and the distances between them, are not shown to scale.

Sunlight

Venus's thick atmosphere reflects most of the sunlight that hits it.

Heavy atmosphere

Venus's atmosphere is very thick. It is mainly made of carbon dioxide gas and is so dense that it presses down on the planet's surface like a great weight. Venus also has clouds made of sulfuric acid. These cause rains that would burn any living thing on the surface.

Morning and evening star

At some times of the year, you can easily see Venus with the naked eye, just before sunrise, or just after sunset. Many astronomers call it the morning star or the evening star, depending on what time of the day it appears. After the Sun and Moon, Venus is the brightest thing in the sky.

This image shows mountains on Venus. It was taken by the Magellan space probe.

Venus's atmosphere reflects the Sun's light like a huge mirror. This is why Venus appears so bright in the sky.

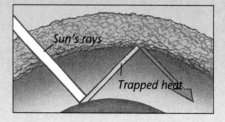

Sun's rays

Trapped heat

Heat from the Sun which does get through the clouds is trapped. On the surface, the temperature can rise to about 480°C (about 900°F).

Slow backspin

Earth's spin   Venus's spin

Venus spins in the opposite direction to the Earth and most other planets.

It takes longer for Venus to rotate once than it does for it to orbit the Sun. This means that on Venus, a day is longer than a year.

Probing Venus

Nobody knew what the surface of Venus looked like until 1975, when two space probes named Venera were sent by the Soviet Union.

Using radar to see through the clouds, the Venera probes mapped the planet's surface. A robot sent to the surface found that it was covered in sharp rocks and looked like a gloomy, orange-brown desert.

Craters

Like Mercury and Mars, Venus has craters, but they are shallower. Venus's thick atmosphere slows down objects which pass through it, so they hit the surface with less force, creating shallower craters.

This dark splodge on Venus was created when an incoming object exploded. The splodge was caused by shock waves from the explosion.

These small craters were formed when shattered pieces of an object fell onto Venus's surface.

Magellan

The American space probe Magellan studied Venus in great detail in the late 1980s and early 90s.

It found that the planet's surface is mostly covered by areas of solidified lava, which has flowed out of the many volcanoes that occur on Venus.

Magellan also found strange cracks and lines which look like spiders' webs. These, known as arachnoids, are only found on Venus, and are thought to have formed when molten rock rose up from below and cracked the crust.

Venus and the Magellan space probe

WARNING!
Always make absolutely sure that the Sun has fully set (in the evening) or has not begun to rise (in the morning) before you look for Venus. You might blind yourself if you glimpse the Sun accidentally through a telescope or binoculars.

This mountain peak is called Gula Mons.

THE EARTH

The Earth orbits the Sun at a speed of about 110,000kmph (almost 70,000mph). It is about 150 million km (around 93 million miles) away from the Sun. Planet Earth takes exactly 365.256 days (one Earth year) to orbit the Sun once.

Mercury *Venus* *Earth*

These planets, and the distances between them, are not shown to scale.

Life on Earth

The Earth's distance from the Sun causes it to have the right temperature for water to exist as a liquid, rather than just as ice or water vapor. Earth also has a breathable atmosphere. Animals and plants need both these things in order to live.

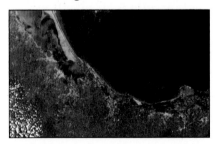

A satellite image of Earth, which has been colored using a computer. In blue, you can see the water, which supports life on Earth. Areas of forest are shown in red. Areas of forest which have been cut down are shown in green.

The atmosphere

The Earth's atmosphere is a mixture of gases that surrounds the planet. It has different layers. Oxygen, which living things use to breathe, makes up about 20% of the atmosphere.

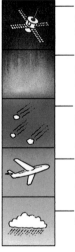

Exosphere. Weather satellites orbit here. It has almost no gases.

Thermosphere. The aurorae (see page 15) are seen in this layer.

Mesosphere. Meteors burn up here.

Stratosphere. Jet planes fly here. It contains the ozone layer, which blocks the Sun's harmful rays.

Troposphere. The weather happens here.

Inside the Earth

Like Mercury, Venus and Mars, the Earth has a rocky crust and a solid metal core. In between the two are different layers.

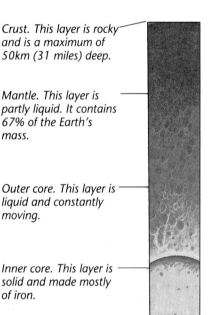

Crust. This layer is rocky and is a maximum of 50km (31 miles) deep.

Mantle. This layer is partly liquid. It contains 67% of the Earth's mass.

Outer core. This layer is liquid and constantly moving.

Inner core. This layer is solid and made mostly of iron.

The Earth's crust is made up of separate pieces, called plates, which rub against one another. They are always moving, sometimes causing earthquakes at the points where they meet.

Looking back at Earth from space

Today, we are learning more and more about our planet from information sent back by satellites and space stations.

Weather forecasters use information collected by satellites to predict weather patterns. They can use this information to warn people of severe weather conditions.

Information from satellites is also used to find out about the Earth's surface. Areas that are normally hard to see, such as the ocean floor, can now be seen in detail.

This satellite picture shows hurricane clouds approaching the east coast of the U.S.A.

This satellite image shows the ridges on the ocean floor between South America and Africa.

Earth in danger

As the world's population grows, we use up more land, and our motor vehicles and industries cause more pollution. This damages the whole environment: the land, oceans and atmosphere.

We need the Earth to provide us with food, water, electricity and materials for use in our everyday lives. It is important to look after the Earth. We can do this by cutting down on pollution and waste, protecting the natural world and recycling old materials.

The picture across the bottom of these pages is a satellite image of Earth, showing Europe, part of Africa and the Persian Gulf.

THE MOON

The Moon orbits the Earth. It is about 384,400km (240,250 miles) away. Most moons are very small compared with the planets that they orbit, but our Moon is large compared with the size of the Earth. It is about a quarter of the Earth's size.

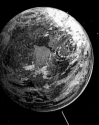

This is what the Earth looks like when seen from the Moon.

The Earth's effect

Earth's gravity makes the Moon spin. It takes the same time for the Moon to spin around once as it does for it to orbit Earth. This means that the same side of the Moon is always facing us.

The Moon spins as it orbits Earth.

In 1969, the U.S. Apollo 11 space mission landed people on the Moon for the first time in history.

An Apollo astronaut exploring the Moon.

Massive craters

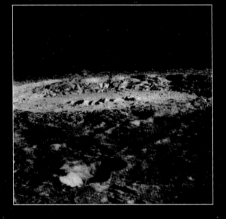

The photograph above shows Copernicus, one of the Moon's craters. It is so large that a city the size of London could fit inside it.

The Moon's craters were made by meteorites hitting it. On a clear night, when the Moon is full, you can see big craters such as Copernicus with the naked eye.

Many of the Moon's craters are surrounded by pale-looking lines, called rays. The rays were made by dust that was thrown out when the meteorites landed.

Seas on the Moon?

There are lots of dark patches on the Moon's surface. These are flat areas of lava which has cooled and become solid. The lava originally poured out of volcanoes.

From the Earth, these flat areas look like seas. Early astronomers called them *mares* (pronounced *mar-ays*), which means "seas" in Latin.

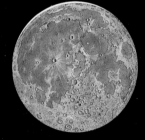

The dark patches on the Moon's surface are the seas.

Mountains

The Moon's surface is very mountainous. The highest range of mountains is called the Apennines. One of its peaks is nearly as high as Mount Everest, the highest mountain on Earth.

This picture shows the side of the Moon that always faces away from Earth.

Temperatures

On Earth, the atmosphere works like a roof. It stops the Sun from making things too hot during the day. At night, it prevents heat from escaping.

The Moon has no atmosphere to protect it. The Sun's rays can make the temperature rise to 123°C (253°F), which is hotter than boiling water.

When the Sun is not shining on the Moon, the temperature can fall to -123°C (-206°F). This is colder than anywhere on Earth.

Phases of the Moon

The Moon does not make its own light, but it reflects the Sun's rays. It can look very bright in the night sky.

The shape of the Moon seems to change from night to night. This is because, as the Moon orbits the Earth, different amounts of its sunlit side are visible. The different shapes are called the phases of the Moon.

It takes 28 days for the Moon to orbit the Earth once. The diagram on the right shows how the Moon's phases occur.

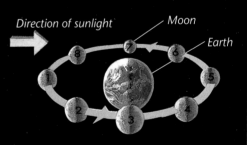

Direction of sunlight   *Moon*   *Earth*

The pictures below show what the Moon looks like from Earth when it is in each of the numbered positions shown above.

1. New moon   5. Full moon

2. Crescent   6. Waning

3. Half moon   7. Half moon

4. Waxing   8. Crescent

MARS

Mars is the fourth planet from the Sun, orbiting at about 225 million km (140 million miles). Mars takes nearly 687 days to orbit the Sun. This is almost twice as long as it takes Earth to do the same.

Mars is only about half the size of Earth.

Mercury Venus Earth Mars

These planets, and the distances between them, are not shown to scale.

Looking at Mars

Mars is visible with the naked eye. It looks like a bright, orange-red star. To see any features on its surface, you need to use a powerful telescope.

Two moons

Mars's moons, Phobos and Deimos, are both dark, dusty and irregular in shape. Phobos orbits Mars at just 6,000km (3,730 miles). Deimos orbits at 20,000km (12,500 miles).

Deimos, Mars's smaller moon, is about 15km (9 miles) across at its widest.

Many scientists think that the oddly-shaped moons are really asteroids that became trapped in orbit around Mars millions of years ago.

Phobos is 28km (17 miles) across at its widest. It has a large crater on it, called Stickney. The crater is about 5km (around 3 miles) across.

The surface of Mars. It is cold, dusty and marked with many craters and canyons.

On the surface

Mars is extremely dusty. The soil contains large amounts of iron, which gives the planet a rusty look. Up close, the landscape looks like bleak orange sand dunes, scattered with thousands of rocks.

Huge storms often rage across Mars, blasting dust over its surface. The storms can last for weeks.

This sunset on Mars was taken during the Mars Pathfinder Mission.

Water for life?

Space probes have photographed deep channels on Mars, which suggest that water once flowed there. In the distant past, Mars may have had rivers and oceans.

Water is essential for plants and animals to live. So if there was water on Mars, then living things may have been able to exist there.

This dry channel on Mars may once have been a flowing river.

Martian meteorite

In 1984, a meteorite landed on Earth. The meteorite was analyzed by scientists in 1996. They decided that it almost certainly originated from Mars, due to the chemical nature of the rock.

Mariner 4

These scientists claim that the meteorite contains fossils of microscopic bacteria-like creatures that lived millions of years ago. If true, this would prove that there were once some simple forms of life on Mars.

Other scientists, however, doubt this theory. Instead, they claim that the remains are not of living things, but of other chemical material.

Investigating Mars

The first successful space probes to go to Mars were the Mariner space probes, in the 1960s. Then, in the 1970s, the Viking probes sent back detailed photographs of the surface.

Pathfinder Mission

In December 1996, the Mars Pathfinder Mission was launched to find out more about Mars. In July 1997, the spacecraft landed on Mars. A remote-controlled vehicle, called the surface rover, was sent to travel over the planet's surface.

The surface rover, known as Sojourner.

JUPITER

Jupiter is the largest planet in the Solar System. It orbits the Sun at a distance of 778 million km (483 million miles). It is so large that over 1,000 planets the size of Earth could fit into it. Astronomers have counted 16 moons orbiting Jupiter, but there may be more.

Mercury   Venus   Earth   Mars   Jupiter

These planets, and the distances between them, are not shown to scale.

Great balls of gas

Jupiter is one of four planets that are made mostly of gas. The others are Saturn, Uranus and Neptune. Together, they are called the gas giants.

Jupiter is so vast that it exerts an enormous gravitational pull on things around it. Asteroids and meteoroids that come near it are sucked into its atmosphere. Jupiter is like a giant vacuum cleaner in space, sucking up pieces of space debris.

Looking at Jupiter

After the Sun, Moon and Venus, Jupiter is the brightest object in the sky. You can see it easily with the naked eye as a bright star. Using a good telescope, you can see its tinted cloud bands and the famous Great Red Spot.

The Galileo space probe made a detailed study of Jupiter.

The Great Red Spot

The Great Red Spot is a huge storm 8km (5 miles) high, 40,000km (25,000 miles) long and 14,000km (8,700 miles) wide. Its winds blow at about 500kmph (310mph).

As the spot moves around, it swallows up other storms. But it is shrinking. It is only half as big as it was 100 years ago.

Jupiter's Great Red Spot

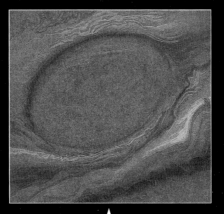

Probing Jupiter

Several space probes have been sent to Jupiter.

Pioneer 10

The first, Pioneer 10, was sent by the U.S.A. in 1972. It reached Jupiter in 1973 and beamed amazing pictures of Jupiter's clouds back to Earth.

Voyagers

In 1979, the Voyager probes discovered that Jupiter has three very faint rings, too fine to be seen from Earth.

Galileo

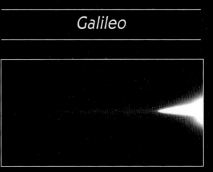

This is a Galileo image of Jupiter's faint outer ring, known as the gossamer ring.

In 1995, the Galileo space probe took a new series of photos of Jupiter. It also sent a mini-probe down into the atmosphere. One of the things it found out was that the winds on Jupiter blew far stronger than any winds on Earth. Galileo also gathered information on Jupiter's rings.

This picture shows what scientists think Jupiter's structure may be.

1 *The atmosphere's top layer is broken by high winds into vast clouds. It forms a beautiful blend of red, brown, orange and yellow.*

2 *The dark bands are gaps in the clouds. You can see through them to deeper, hotter layers of the planet's churning atmosphere.*

3 *This layer is 17,000km (10,565 miles) thick. Made of hydrogen gas, it is so compressed that it behaves like liquid.*

4 *This layer is also made of hydrogen. It is even more compressed and behaves like a solid. It is so heavy that it makes up over 77% of Jupiter's mass.*

5 *The core is solid and rocky. It is slightly larger than Earth.*

Ganymede is the largest moon in the Solar System. It is even larger than the planet Mercury.

Many moons

So far, astronomers have discovered 16 moons around Jupiter. The four largest (shown here*) are called the Galilean Moons after the Italian scientist Galileo, who discovered them in 1610. You can see these moons with binoculars.

Jupiter's other moons are much smaller, and some may be just asteroids, or debris from a moon that was destroyed.

Europa. A deep ocean beneath the icy crust may hold simple life forms. Many scientists think that there is a greater chance of finding life on Jupiter's moons than anywhere else in the Solar System.

Callisto. This moon is basically a ball of dusty ice. It is scarred with hundreds of craters that make it look similar to Earth's moon.

Io (below) is covered with volcanoes that pour sulfur onto the surface.

Europa's icy surface, shown here in blue.

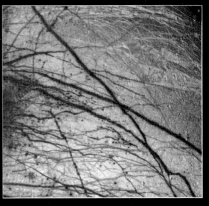

*The Galilean Moons are not shown to scale

SATURN

Saturn is the second largest planet in the Solar System. It is often called the ringed planet because it is surrounded by distinctive rings of dust and rocks. Lying about 1,425 million km (890 million miles) from the Sun, Saturn orbits once every 29 Earth years.

Earth

This image of Saturn was taken by the Hubble Space Telescope and beamed back through space. Compare Saturn with the size of the Earth, shown above it.

Mercury   Venus   Earth   Mars   Jupiter   Saturn

These planets, and the distances between them, are not shown to scale.

Saturn's moons

Saturn has 18 moons – even more than Jupiter. Here are details of some of them.

Second biggest

Saturn is smaller than Jupiter, but it is still enormous. It measures about 119,300km (74,130 miles) across – nine times wider than the Earth.

Gas giant

Like Jupiter, Saturn is a gas giant. It is made up mostly of hydrogen. Its atmosphere also contains a lot of helium, which is a very light gas. This makes Saturn a relatively light planet. In fact, if you could find an ocean that was big enough to drop Saturn into, the planet would float.

Astronomers believe that inside, Saturn may be similar to Jupiter.

Spinning planet

Saturn spins very quickly, taking just ten hours to go around. As a result of this fast spin, the gases in its atmosphere are flung out toward its equator – the imaginary line around Saturn's middle.

Saturn bulges out in the region of its equator.

The gases bulge out, making Saturn fatter in the middle. You can see this even through a home telescope.

Mimas is 390km (244 miles) wide and covered in craters. The impact that created its largest crater nearly destroyed it. Its nickname is the "Death Star".

Enceladus is slightly larger than Mimas and is much smoother. Most of its craters are covered by ice.

Tethys has massive craters and long valleys. The longest valley, Ithaca, is 2,000km (1,243 miles) long. Its largest crater, Odysseus, is 400km (240 miles) wide.

Saturn's biggest moon is Titan, which has a thick atmosphere. It is even bigger than the planet Mercury. Some astronomers think that it may be able to support life.

Early observations

Early astronomers, using their unsophisticated telescopes, could not see Saturn's rings in much detail. In fact, when the seventeenth century Italian astronomer Galileo first saw them, he thought that he was seeing three planets in a row. Later, he became convinced that Saturn had rings around it.

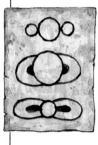

Here are some drawings Galileo made of his early observations of Saturn. They show how he first mistook the rings for planets.

This amazing Voyager 2 image of Saturn's rings was downloaded from one of NASA's websites on the Internet.

Saturn's rings

Space probes have sent back lots of information about Saturn's rings. The first space probe to visit Saturn was Pioneer 11. In 1979, it sent photographs of Saturn back to Earth. Later, the Voyager expeditions revealed even more.

★ Saturn's rings are only about 1km (less than a mile) thick. They are made up of particles that range in size from specks of dust to large, icy boulders.

Pioneer 11

★ The rings that are visible from Earth are in fact made up of thousands of smaller ones, called ringlets. The two outermost ringlets are twisted around each other, like strands in a rope.

★ The outer ring particles are kept in place by the gravity of two small moons which orbit Saturn. These are called the Shepherd Moons.

★ Clouds of fine dust, looking like the spokes of a wheel, rotate around Saturn above one of its rings. It is now possible to see these spokes through powerful telescopes.

Disappearing rings

As Saturn and Earth go around the Sun, our view of the rings changes. This is because Saturn lies on a slight tilt (just like Earth and most other planets) so that its rings are also at a tilt.

When Saturn's angle of tilt is sideways to the Earth, the rings almost disappear.

When the top of Saturn is pointing toward us, the rings look like this.

When the top of Saturn is pointing away from us, the rings look like this.

URANUS

U ranus is the seventh planet from the Sun, lying at a distance of around 2,900 million km (around 1,800 million miles). It takes just over 84 Earth years to orbit the Sun. It was first identified as a planet by the British astronomer William Herschel in 1781.

Ariel

Mercury Venus Earth Mars Jupiter Saturn Uranus

These planets, and the distances between them, are not shown to scale.

Seeing Uranus

At its brightest, Uranus can be glimpsed with the naked eye if you know just where to look. Like the other planets, though, it appears to change its position among the stars. It looks like a star, although it does not twinkle.

Strange spin

Uranus spins on its side. No other planet does this. Many astronomers think that its unusual spin is the result of a collision with a planet-sized object millions of years ago.

Uranus's rings

Like Saturn and Jupiter, Uranus has rings. They were first discovered from Earth in 1977. Then, in 1986, the Voyager space probe photographed and measured them. Mostly, the rings are made up of dust. The outer ring's dust is particularly dark.

Uranus

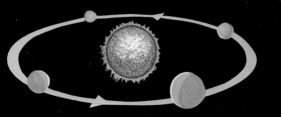

This picture shows Uranus rolling on its side as it orbits the Sun.

Umbriel

Titania

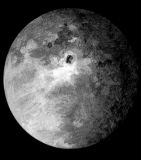

Oberon

Miranda

What Uranus is made of

The atmosphere of Uranus is mostly hydrogen gas, with helium and tiny amounts of other gases. The upper atmosphere contains a lot of helium, which makes Uranus look blue-green. The planet has a small, rocky core.

Spinning and orbiting

Uranus spins quickly, taking just 18 hours to make one complete turn. Earth takes 24 hours to spin once, but Uranus is far larger, so at its cloud tops it moves far faster than the Earth.

In its orbit of the Sun, Uranus moves through space at about 7km (4¼ miles) per second. In comparison, the Earth moves at nearly 30km (19 miles) per second.

Moons around Uranus

Uranus has at least 15 moons, although there may be more that are yet to be discovered.

Its five biggest moons are shown above. Ariel and Umbriel are both dark and cratered, while Titania has deep, long valleys. Oberon is heavily cratered, but little else is known about this moon. Miranda is a small ball of battered ice, only 472km (293 miles) across. It is thought that it may once have been broken apart by a comet.

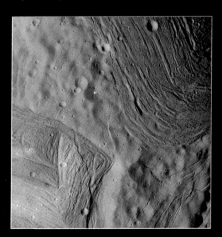

This grooved feature (bottom left) on Miranda, is known as the Chevron.

NEPTUNE

Neptune was first identified as a planet in 1846 by the German astronomer Johann Gottfried Galle. Neptune is the fourth of the gas giants. It is slightly smaller than Uranus. It spins once every 16 hours.

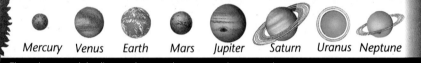

Mercury   Venus   Earth   Mars   Jupiter   Saturn   Uranus   Neptune

These planets, and the distances between them, are not shown to scale.

Distant planet

Neptune is over 4,500 million km (about 2,800 million miles) from the Sun. It is so far away that it takes nearly 165 Earth years to orbit the Sun.

Neptune cannot be seen with the naked eye, and through binoculars it looks like a star. Powerful telescopes show it as a small, bluish circle.

Featureless

Because it is so far from Earth, astronomers had, until recently, been unable to see Neptune in detail. They assumed that Neptune would be a rather dull-looking planet. However, the space probe Voyager 2's cameras proved that it is similar to the other gas giants. For instance, fierce storms rage across its surface.

Dark spots

Several dark spots have been seen on Neptune. The largest, about the size of Earth, is called the Great Dark Spot. It may be a gigantic storm, like the Great Red Spot on Jupiter.

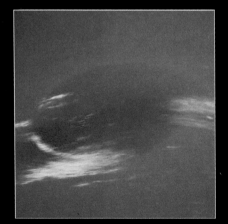

The Great Dark Spot, shown above, was first seen by the Voyager 2 probe in 1989. But in the 1990s, the Hubble Space Telescope could not find it. Nobody is sure why the Great Dark Spot vanished, or whether it will reappear.

A photo of Neptune, taken by the Voyager 2 space probe in 1989.

Blue planet

Neptune's bluish appearance comes from the methane gas in its atmosphere, which has a blue color. Neptune's atmosphere also contains hydrogen, helium and water.

Beneath its dense, thick, cloudy atmosphere, Neptune is thought to be made up of a mixture of molten rock, water, liquid ammonia and methane.

Neptune's moons

Neptune has eight moons. The biggest of them are Triton and Nereid. Triton is even bigger than the planet Pluto. Unlike most moons, it orbits in the opposite direction to Neptune's spin, as shown below.

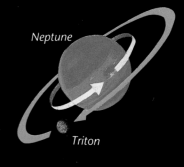

Neptune

Triton

Most of Triton's surface is bright and smooth. It has some dark streaks over its surface and pink ice around its south pole. It has a thin atmosphere.

This photo of Triton shows the smooth part of its surface on the left. A more pitted area is shown on the right. It was taken by the Voyager 2 space probe.

Stormy surface

Long, wispy clouds race around Neptune. They are blown by the fastest winds found on any planet in the Solar System. Near the Great Dark Spot, the winds blow at up to 2,000kmph (1,200mph).

One cloud zooms around Neptune once every 16 hours. Scientists have nicknamed this cloud the Scooter, because it scoots over the planet so quickly.

Almost all our knowledge of Neptune came from the Voyager 2 space probe's fly-past in 1989. Voyager 2 found several incomplete rings around Neptune. They were so dark that nobody could see them from Earth.

PLUTO

Most of the time, Pluto is the most distant planet from the Sun. It has an oval-shaped orbit, though, which takes it closer to the Sun than Neptune for 20 years of its 249-year orbit. As a result, during 1979-1999, Neptune was the most distant planet from the Sun.

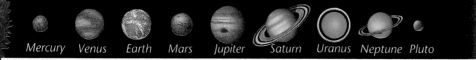

Mercury   Venus   Earth   Mars   Jupiter   Saturn   Uranus   Neptune   Pluto

These planets, and the distances between them, are not shown to scale.

Far away and hard to see

Pluto's distance from the Sun varies a great deal. At its closest, it is 4,425 million km (2,750 million miles) from the Sun. At its farthest, it is 7,375 million km (4,583 million miles) away. Because Pluto is so far away, it is very hard to see from Earth.

Even powerful telescopes on Earth show Pluto as just a tiny circle with no surface markings. But Hubble Space Telescope photographs suggest that it may look like Neptune's moon, Triton. Pluto's diameter is around 2,300km (1,429 miles), slightly smaller than Triton.

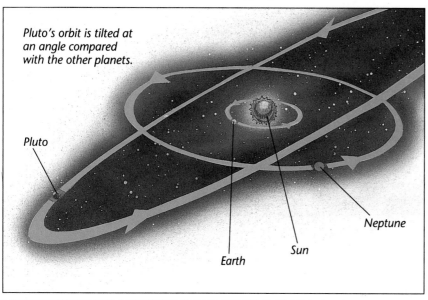

Pluto's orbit is tilted at an angle compared with the other planets.

Pluto

Neptune

Sun

Earth

Finding Pluto

The planets pull at one another, affecting the shapes of each other's orbits. Before Pluto was discovered, astronomers thought that Uranus and Neptune were being pulled by a planet beyond Neptune that they couldn't see. Then, in 1930, Pluto was discovered by an American named Clyde Tombaugh.

Another planet?

Astronomers now know that Pluto is too small to affect the orbits of Uranus and Neptune to any great extent. Some scientists believe there is a tenth planet out there, yet to be discovered. This mystery planet is nicknamed Planet X.

Pluto and its single moon, Charon.

Pluto's moon

Pluto has only one moon, called Charon. It was discovered in 1978 when astronomers examining a photo of Pluto noticed that it looked stretched out. More detailed photographs showed that Pluto actually had a single large moon.

Charon is unusually large for a moon. It is nearly half as big as Pluto. Because of this, many astronomers think that Pluto and Charon are really a pair of planets.

Close together

○-●

Pluto and Charon

● - ○

Earth   *Moon*

In space terms, Charon and Pluto are very close to one another. They are only about 20,000km (12,000 miles) apart. The Earth and the Moon are about 384,000km (239,000 miles) apart.

Pluto and Charon, as seen through the Hubble Space Telescope.

Pluto's atmosphere

Photographs suggest that Pluto has a surface of frozen methane and nitrogen. It may also have a thin atmosphere. Its poles are brighter than its other regions.

Scientists think that as Pluto moves away from the Sun, its atmosphere may freeze solid and fall to the planet's surface. NASA plans to send a probe, the Pluto Express, to study the atmosphere before it freezes. It may be launched early in the twenty-first century.

Planet X

Many scientists think that if it exists, Planet X must be bigger than Pluto. But it has never been found. It may be too far away to find – perhaps twice as far from the Sun as Pluto. Also, its orbit could take it way above and below the orbits of the other planets.

Some small objects have been found beyond Pluto. The objects may form part of a ring of icy bodies, called the Kuiper Belt by astronomers.

The Kuiper Belt theory makes the existence of Planet X less likely, because these small objects may account for the pull on Uranus and Neptune.

Pluto

Kuiper Belt

One of the icy bodies in the Kuiper Belt, nicknamed Smiley.

ASTEROIDS

A steroids are large pieces of either rock, or rock and metal. Scientists believe that they are the bits and pieces that were left over when our Solar System formed 5,000 million years ago.

The first sighting

In 1801, an Italian astronomer named Piazzi spotted an object in space through his telescope. At first, he thought it was a small planet. Piazzi named his discovery Ceres.

Soon, other astronomers noticed similar objects. They shone at night like faint stars, so they were named *asteroids*, which means "like stars".

Close-up first

The first close-up pictures of an asteroid were taken in 1991, by the space probe Galileo. It photographed the asteroid Gaspra.

The images showed Gaspra to be more than 20km (12 miles) across and irregular in shape. It is grooved, and pitted with craters. A picture of Gaspra is shown below.

The space probe Galileo showed Gaspra to be dark reddish-brown, with patches of gray and blue. It may be two asteroids joined into one by a collision.

Killer asteroid

Very rarely, asteroids collide with the Earth, leaving large craters. Scientists think that a massive asteroid slammed into the Earth 65 million years ago, causing more damage than thousands of nuclear bombs.

The site of the impact is thought to be the Chicxulub* Crater in Mexico.

It is possible that the force of this asteroid caused tidal waves in the sea and fires over the land that blotted out the sunlight for years. Many types of plants and animals, including the dinosaurs, died out.

*Pronounced "chick-shu-lub".

The Asteroid Belt

Most asteroids orbit the Sun between Mars and Jupiter, in a region called the Asteroid Belt. In the twenty-first century, space probes will be studying them more closely.

How many?

Astronomers have so far recorded the orbits of around 4,000 asteroids. But they think that there could be well over 10,000 asteroids that are over 100km (62 miles) across, and an even greater number of smaller ones.

The distances between asteroids in the Asteroid Belt are so massive that spacecraft can pass through without hitting any of them.

Different types

Although there are many thousands of asteroids, they fall into three main groups depending on what they are made of. The groups are carbonaceous (like Ceres), silicaceous (like Gaspra) and metallic asteroids.

Carbonaceous asteroids are common. They are stony and darker than coal.

Silicaceous asteroids are bright, stony bodies, which contain metal.

Metallic asteroids may be the exposed, metallic cores of much larger bodies.

Trojan asteroids

Jupiter holds clusters of asteroids in its gravity. As it spins around the Sun, some asteroids sit in front of its orbit, while others sit behind. These asteroids are called the Trojans.

Other asteroids, known as the Apollo asteroids, sometimes cross the Earth's path. Their usual orbit, however, is farther away from the Sun.

Apollo

Trojans

Earth

Jupiter

Trojans

COMETS AND METEORS

Compared with the Sun and the planets of the Solar System, comets and meteors are small. Scientists believe that, like asteroids, they are pieces of debris left over from when the Solar System formed. They are like pieces of space litter that whizz around the Solar System. Occasionally, you can see them from Earth.

One of the longest comet tails ever recorded was that of the Great Comet of 1843. It was about 330 million km (about 200 million miles) long.

Comets

Comets are chunks of dirty ice mixed with dust and grit. They have oval-shaped orbits, so they spend most of their time far from the Sun and only come near it for a brief time.

The comet's icy nucleus is hidden in here.

Tail

Coma

Glowing tail

The solid part of a comet (the nucleus) is surrounded by a cloud of glowing gases, called the coma.

The coma stretches out into a tail that can become broken up into streamers, with delicate twists and swirls.

How big?

Most comets have a nucleus that is less than 10km (about 6 miles) wide.

As a comet approaches the Sun, the coma can be as long as 80,000km (50,000 miles), with a tail of over 1 million km (600,000 miles).

Seeing a comet

Comets can be seen from Earth only when they are fairly near to the Sun. Most look like smudges of light, even through telescopes.

Some comets have very long orbits which take them far out into the rest of the Solar System. They may only be seen from Earth once every few thousand years. Comets with shorter orbits can be seen more often and it is easier to predict their return.

Between 1995 and 1997, comet Hale-Bopp came into view. It was the clearest comet for nearly a hundred years. Its nucleus may be as wide as 40km (25 miles).

When a comet is far away from the Sun, it all remains solid. It has no tail and it speeds through space like a dirty snowball.

As the comet nears the Sun, the Sun's rays start to melt it. Gas and dust begin to stream out into space forming a cloud which is called the coma.

A constant stream of particles from the Sun, called the solar wind, blows some of the coma out behind it to form a spectacular tail.

Entering the atmosphere

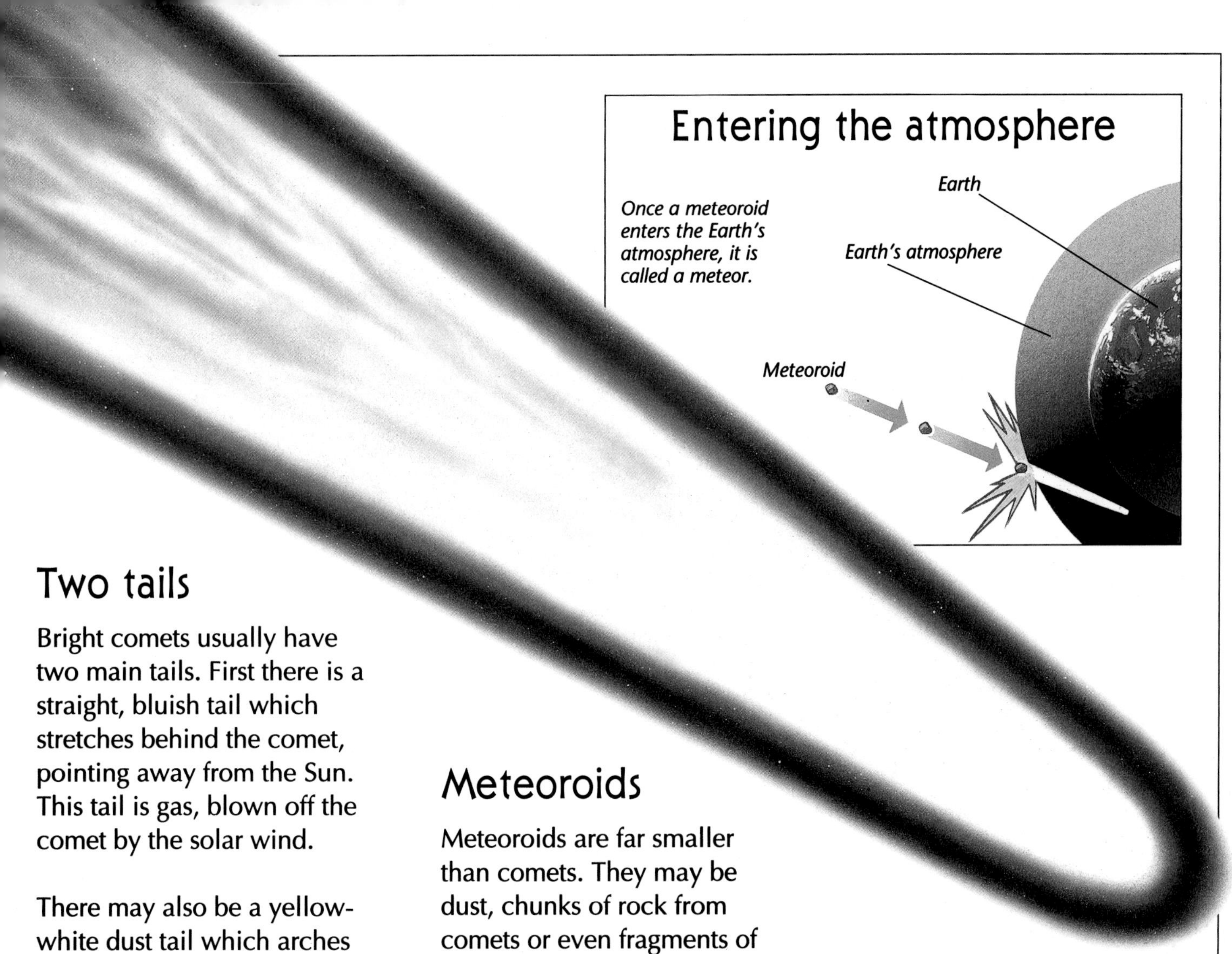

Once a meteoroid enters the Earth's atmosphere, it is called a meteor.

Earth

Earth's atmosphere

Meteoroid

Two tails

Bright comets usually have two main tails. First there is a straight, bluish tail which stretches behind the comet, pointing away from the Sun. This tail is gas, blown off the comet by the solar wind.

There may also be a yellow-white dust tail which arches out in another direction. This traces out the path of the comet's orbit.

Some comets have more than two tails. A comet known as De Chéseaux comet had seven, fanning out like a peacock's tail.

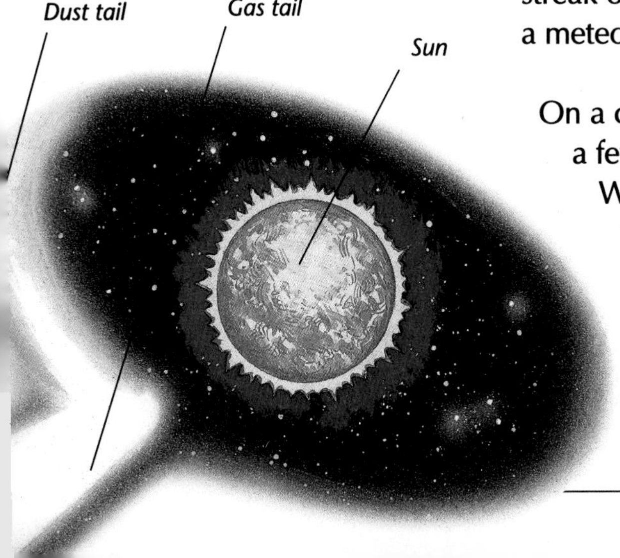

Dust tail

Gas tail

Sun

Meteoroids

Meteoroids are far smaller than comets. They may be dust, chunks of rock from comets or even fragments of shattered asteroids.

Shooting stars

When the Earth crosses the paths of these meteoroids, they burn up as they plummet through the Earth's atmosphere. They make a streak of light which is called a meteor, or a shooting star.

On a clear night you can see a few meteors every hour. When Earth passes through a stream of dust left behind by a comet, dozens of meteors may be seen every hour during one night.

Space stones

Some pieces of meteors survive their fiery plunge through the Earth's atmosphere. They fall to the Earth as charred rocks. Once they hit the ground, these rocks are called meteorites. They are usually dark and very heavy, often looking rusty in places.

Scientists study meteorites because they provide samples of rocks from outer space. Most meteorites have been found to consist of rock, iron, or a mixture of both.

EXPLORING SPACE

Scientists have been sending rockets up into space since the late 1950s in an effort to learn more about the universe. Since then, many missions have been funded by the U.S.A. and Russia (the Soviet Union before 1992), which have vastly increased our knowledge.

Skylab

Space explorers

The most exciting and attention-grabbing explorations took place between 1968 and 1972, when astronauts from the U.S.A. journeyed to the Moon on the Apollo missions.

In 1969, during the Apollo 11 mission, Neil Armstrong and Buzz Aldrin became the first people ever to set foot on the Moon.

The Apollo 11 moon mission blasts off from Cape Kennedy, July 16, 1969. Today, Cape Kennedy is officially called the Kennedy Space Center.

Space stations

Space stations orbit the Earth at a distance of about 400km (250 miles). They are laboratories where experiments can be done unaffected by Earth's gravity.

The U.S.A.'s first space station was Skylab, launched in 1973. Mir, the largest Russian space station, was launched in 1986. It is designed to have specially made pieces, called modules, attached to it or removed from it in space. These are purpose-built according to their use.

Living in space

Astronauts may stay on space stations for several months. This helps to find out what the effects of space are on the human body – and how to counteract them. This knowledge will be vital for the health of astronauts on the long journeys planned to Mars for the twenty-first century.

Mir in trouble

In June 1997, Mir suffered a collision with a supply ship. Its power supply was damaged and the astronauts were forced to save power until repairs could be made by a replacement crew.

The picture below shows the Mir space station in orbit around the Earth.

Satellites

There are many man-made objects, called satellites, in orbit around the Earth. Some gather and transmit information about space to scientists on Earth. Others, called communication satellites, pick up radio, TV or telephone signals from Earth, and send them back down to other places on the globe.

Sputnik

The first man-made object ever to go into space was a satellite launched by the Soviet Union on October 4, 1957.

Officially named "Satellite 1957 Alpha 2", it carried a small, beeping transmitter. It became better known by its nickname, Sputnik, which is a Russian word meaning "little voyager".

Hipparcos

In 1989, the satellite Hipparcos was launched by the European Space Agency. For three and a half years, it mapped the night sky in the finest detail ever. Results were published in 1997 and this new information allowed astronomers to calculate how far away thousands of stars and other objects are with greater accuracy than ever.

Planet probing

Since the 1960s, space probes have been sent to explore the Solar System. They have beamed back masses of new information about the planets. One ingenious project was NASA's Galileo mission to Jupiter, launched in 1989. Part of Galileo was a smaller probe (shown below) which split from its mother ship to study the planet's atmosphere.

As predicted by scientists, the Galileo probe was destroyed as it completed its studies of Jupiter's stormy clouds.

Pioneer 10 (which studied Jupiter) and Pioneer 11 (Saturn) have journeyed farther than any other probes. After completing their missions, they coasted far away from our solar system.

The central part of the Galileo probe, packed with atmospheric sensors and other scientific instruments.

This section shielded the probe's delicate measuring instruments as it plunged into Jupiter's atmosphere.

FAMOUS ASTRONOMERS

Ptolemy

Born: AD120, Greece
Died: AD180
Listed many of the star constellations. Said that the Sun and planets all revolved around the Earth. His ideas were accepted as true for the next 1,400 years.

Nicholas Copernicus

Born: 1473, Poland
Died: 1543
Developed a theory that the planets revolved around the Sun. His ideas caused a great scientific and religious debate.

Tycho Brahe

Born: 1546, Denmark
Died: 1601
Observed a supernova (see page 53) in 1572. Although he suspected that Copernicus's ideas were correct, his strong religious beliefs meant that he tried to prove Copernicus wrong. He never did.

Galileo Galilei

Born: 1564, Italy
Died: 1642
Using the recently-invented telescope, sketched pictures of the Moon, Saturn's rings and four of Jupiter's moons. Proved Copernicus's theory.

Johannes Kepler

Born: 1571, Germany
Died: 1630
Published three laws of planetary motion between 1609 and 1619. Regarded as one of the founders of modern astronomy.

Isaac Newton

Born: 1643, England
Died: 1727
Discovered the law of gravity, showing that the movement of the stars and planets could be predicted. Astronomy became much more accurate.

William Herschel

Born: 1738, Germany
Died: 1822
Discovered Uranus in March 1781, using a homemade telescope. His discovery revealed that the Solar System was far larger than anybody had previously thought.

Albert Einstein

Born: 1879, Germany
Died: 1955
Revolutionized science in the early twentieth century with his theories and findings in the subject of physics. His ideas changed the way that scientists thought about and studied the universe.

Edwin Hubble

Born: 1889, U.S.A.
Died: 1953
Revealed that the universe is far larger than had been thought. Put forward early ideas of the Big Bang theory.

Clyde Tombaugh

Born: 1906, U.S.A.
Died: 1997
Discovered Pluto, the ninth and most distant planet of the Solar System, in 1930.

Arno Penzias and Robert Wilson

Penzias born: 1933, Germany
Wilson born: 1936, U.S.A.
Found evidence of the Big Bang explosion, adding more weight to Hubble's theory.

Carl Sagan

Born: 1935, U.S.A.
Died: 1997
A great popularizer of astronomy, who wrote several best-selling books and TV series on astronomy.

Stephen Hawking

Born: 1942, England
Widely thought to be the most brilliant scientist since Einstein. Best known for his work on black holes.

THE STARS

An astronomer watches the stars, with the Milky Way in the sky above.

STAR GROUPS

Stars are not randomly sprinkled throughout the universe. They are grouped in galaxies, each of which contains billions of stars. Our Solar System forms a tiny part of a galaxy called the Milky Way.

Galaxies

Galaxies form in different shapes. Four of the most common shapes are: spiral, barred spiral, elliptical and irregular (see right).

A third of all known galaxies are spiral shaped. Most astronomers agree that the Milky Way is a spiral.

Recently, astronomers using sophisticated telescopes have found new galaxies that are bigger and less tightly packed with stars than any they have seen before. They don't give off much light, so they are known as low surface brightness galaxies.

A spiral galaxy. It has a bright middle and two or more curved arms of stars.

A barred spiral has a central bar with an arm at each end.

An elliptical galaxy. It has masses of old, red stars which contain little gas or dust. Elliptical galaxies vary in shape from circular to oval.

An irregular galaxy. This kind of galaxy doesn't really have any fixed shape. They are just like clouds of stars.

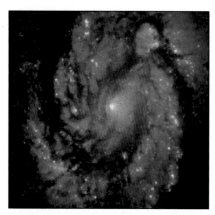

The spiral galaxy M100. It is 30 million light years away from Earth.

Nearest galaxies

The galaxies closest to our Milky Way are the Large and Small Magellanic Clouds. These are small, irregular galaxies. The nearest large galaxy after them is the Andromeda Galaxy. This spiral galaxy is the most distant object visible with the naked eye. It is 2.9* million light years away.

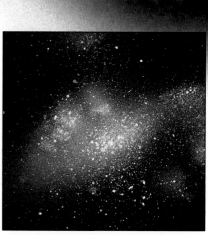

The Large Magellanic Cloud (middle) and the Small Magellanic Cloud (top).

This figure is taken from the Hipparcos satellite readings – see page 43.

Seeing galaxies

When you look at a galaxy, you see the combined light of its billions of stars. Through small telescopes, most galaxies appear as smudges of light. They can be seen much more clearly through powerful telescopes.

Galactic groups

Galaxies are not just scattered around the universe, they are grouped together in clusters. Our cluster, called the Local Group, is relatively small, containing about 30 galaxies stretching across 5 million light years.

Star clusters

Inside galaxies, stars tend to group together in clusters. There are two types of star clusters. Open clusters, such as the one shown below, are made up of bright young stars which have just formed and are still relatively close together in space.

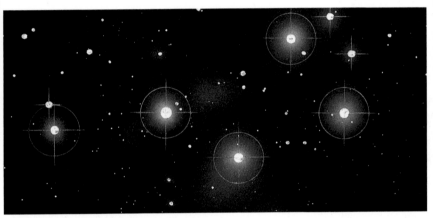

The Pleiades group of stars, in the constellation Taurus, is an open cluster.

Globular clusters are much larger than open clusters. They tend to be found above and below the central bulge of a galaxy. There are about 150 known globular clusters in our galaxy, each containing up to a million stars.

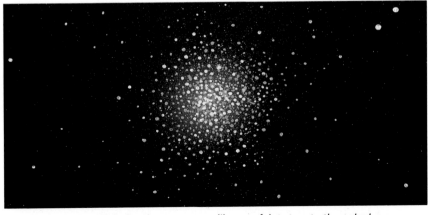

A globular cluster. Globular clusters appear like very faint stars to the naked eye.

A Hubble Space Telescope image of the Cartwheel Galaxy in the Sculptor constellation. It is 500 million light years away.

Space collision

The Cartwheel Galaxy, above, is an enormous galaxy, 150,000 light years across. Its rare shape was formed when a smaller galaxy smashed into it. The outer ring is an immense circle of gas and dust which expanded from the core after the collision. Its original spiral shape is now starting to re-form.

THE MILKY WAY

The Earth and the Solar System are located here in the Milky Way.

Compared with other galaxies, our galaxy, the Milky Way, is relatively large. It measures approximately 100,000 light years across. The Earth and the rest of our Solar System lie about 28,000 light years from the middle of the Milky Way.

Rotating spiral

Most astronomers are convinced that the Milky Way is a spiral galaxy. Some, though, have suggested that it might be a barred spiral galaxy instead.

Like all spiral and barred spiral galaxies, the Milky Way rotates. Closer to the middle it rotates faster than at its edges. Our Solar System revolves around the middle of the galaxy about once every 225 million years. According to this theory, the Solar System has only rotated once since the earliest dinosaurs walked the Earth.

Seeing the galaxy

On a clear night, you can see a broad, dense band of stars which stretches across the sky. In ancient times, people thought this band looked like a trail of spilled milk. This is how our galaxy gets its name. When you look along this band, you are looking toward the middle of the Milky Way.

The Milky Way. Through binoculars, you can see some of the millions of stars that make up this galaxy.

At least 150 huge globular star clusters hover above and below the middle of the galaxy. Each contains up to a million stars.

Areas of glowing pink, blue and green gas are nebulae, the regions where new stars form.

When to look

If you could see the Milky Way from the side, you would see that it has a central bulge. Its shape looks like a pair of fried eggs placed back to back.

In the northern hemisphere, the best time to see the Milky Way is between the months of July and September. It also looks impressive on dark midwinter nights.

In the southern hemisphere, the Milky Way is seen at its most spectacular between October and December. This is when it looks most like a trail of spilled milk across the sky.

BIRTH OF STARS

Astronomers have pieced together the story of how stars form by observing the many different stars that can be seen from Earth. Stars change throughout their life and eventually die.

A star's birthplace

New stars form within vast clouds of gas and dust, called nebulae. Some nebulae are bright and some are dark. Dark nebulae are made mostly of dust and so they blot out the light of stars behind them. They look like dark patches of starless sky.

Most nebulae can only be seen through a telescope, but you can see the nebula M42, with binoculars. It lies in Orion (see page 69).

Horse's Head Nebula

This dark nebula, called the Horse's Head Nebula, is silhouetted against a bright nebula. The Horse's Head also lies in the constellation Orion. You need a powerful telescope to see this nebula.

Trifid Nebula

This bright nebula is the Trifid Nebula. The gases in it are so hot that they make the surrounding gas clouds glow in beautiful shades. Hydrogen glows pink, while oxygen glows green-blue. You need a good telescope to see it.

These columns of gas and dust are part of M16, the Eagle Nebula.

Starting off

Before stars begin to form in a nebula, the clouds of gases and dust swirl around and around. They then form into clumps which grow larger and larger.

Cloud collapse

Eventually, something causes the clouds to collapse. Some astronomers think that this might happen when the clouds pass through the arms of a spiral galaxy.

Some suggest that the shock wave from an exploding star (a supernova – see page 53) might start the collapse.

This image, taken with the Hubble Space Telescope, shows a nebula in the irregular galaxy NGC 2366. It is 10 million light years away.

The brightest star visible in this nebula may be 60 times as big as the Sun.

Shining star

As the cloud collapses, the temperature rises inside. After tens of thousands of years of collapse, a hot core forms. The core gets hotter and hotter until nuclear reactions begin inside, making the clump of gases start to shine. The new star has been born. Most new stars are hot and bright, but some are cooler and dimmer.

Gases and dust swirl.

The clouds collapse.

A hot core forms.

A new star is born.

A star in middle age.

Our Sun

At first, most new stars burn very brightly. They appear either blue or white. This state continues for millions of years.

As they get older, they settle down and shine less brightly but more steadily, like our Sun. The Sun is only halfway through its lifespan of around 10,000 million years.

LIFE OF A STAR

Stars burn with different brightnesses and colors. The hotter the star, the bluer it shines. Their lifespans are different too. The smaller the star, the longer it tends to live.

The Cat's Eye Nebula. The red and green areas are clouds of dense, glowing gas.

Lifespans

Stars such as our Sun have a lifespan of about 10,000 million years. Stars smaller than our Sun, called dwarf stars, live longer.

Stars larger than our Sun are called giant stars. The biggest of all are called supergiant stars. They have short lives of only a few million years.

Barnard's star, in the constellation Ophiuchus (see page 65), is a red dwarf star, cooler than our Sun.

The Sun is a yellow star.

Arcturus, in the constellation Boötes (see page 63), is an orange giant star.

This diagram compares the size of some bright stars, including our Sun.

Rigel, in the constellation Orion (see page 69), is a hot blue supergiant star.

Death of a star

Eventually a star's supply of gas runs out and it dies. As they die, stars that are the size of our Sun (or smaller) swell up and turn red. They are called red giants.

Slowly they puff their outer layers of gas, called planetary nebulae*, into space.

White dwarf

A small, almost dead star, called a white dwarf, is left. It is about the size of a planet, and is very heavy and dense for its size. Imagine a golf ball that weighs as much as a truck.

Because it is so dense, a white dwarf generates huge gravity. It eventually cools and fades.

*A planetary nebula has nothing to do with planets.

Explosive death

Stars that are bigger than our Sun have a really spectacular death. First they swell into vast red stars, called red supergiants. Then they blow up with a huge explosion, called a supernova.

Four supernovas have been seen in our galaxy in the last thousand years. They glowed brighter than anything else around them for several days before disappearing.

Dense and heavy

The supernova leaves a rapidly expanding layer of gases and dust with a small spinning star in the middle. This is a neutron star. It is even denser and heavier than a white dwarf. (Imagine a golf ball which weighs as much as a skyscraper.)

Some neutron stars send out beams of radiation that swing around as the star spins. These stars are called pulsars.

Black holes

When the very biggest stars die they form red supergiants. Then they explode into a supernova. However, when they collapse, they shrink so much that they virtually vanish from the universe. They may become what are called black holes – bottomless pits from which nothing escapes.

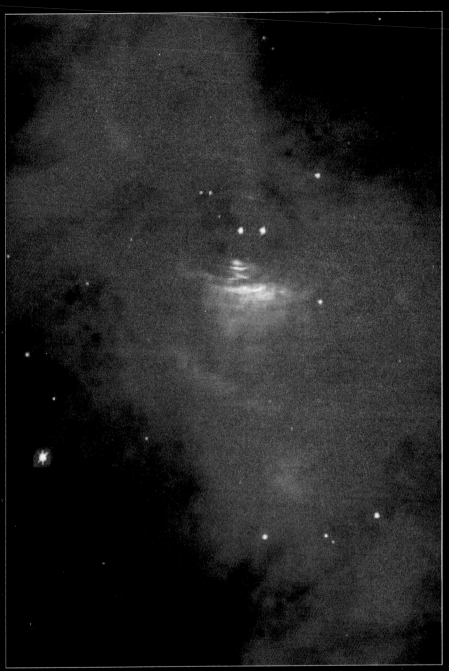

A digital image of the Crab Nebula. This nebula is the remains of a supernova explosion which took place over 900 years ago. It is ten light years across and is located 7,000 light years away in the region of Taurus. At its heart lies the Crab Pulsar – a neutron star.

Sucked in

Compared to the size of stars and planets, black holes are tiny..Many could be only the same size across as a medium-sized town. But they are so heavy and dense that their gravity sucks everything inside them, even light.

This means that we can't see black holes. Anything that goes close to one is likely to be crushed. Some scientists think that in the middle of our galaxy lies an enormous black hole, surrounded by a mass of ancient red stars.

VARIABLE STARS

Some stars appear to change gradually in brilliance. These are called variable stars and they fall into three main types – pulsating variables, eclipsing variables and cataclysmic variables.

Algol, also known as the Demon Star, is the most well-known variable star. It is really two stars which orbit one another, appearing bright and then dim.

Watching variables

You need to watch a variable star over days, weeks or even months to see it go through a full cycle, or period, of changes. It helps to compare the star with a nearby star which is not variable, so that you can tell whether it is getting fainter or brighter.

Some variable stars' cycles are regular and others are more erratic.

March

May

Pulsating variables

Pulsating variables shrink and swell, giving off more light when large and less light when small. They change in size and temperature. They are usually giant or supergiant stars.

The pictures on the right show Mira, a pulsating variable in the constellation Cetus.

July

September

Eclipsing variables

Some variable stars are not single stars at all. These variable stars really consist of two stars, called a binary, or physical double, star. The stars orbit around each other. Their gravity keeps them swinging around one another.

As one star passes in front of the other, it blocks its light. This reduces the amount of light that you can see from Earth.

The brighter star is called the primary.

The fainter star is called the secondary.

Cataclysmic variables

These are binary stars that are very close together. When the gravity of one of them (usually a white dwarf) pulls material away from the other (usually a red giant), a huge and sudden increase in brightness occurs. This is caused by violent nuclear reactions.

Flaring stars

One type of cataclysmic variable is called a nova. It flares suddenly, then it fades back to its original brightness over several months – or even years if it flared really brightly. Novas can be so bright that they can look like new stars.

Novas are fairly uncommon. There are about 25 each year in a galaxy such as ours. Since 1600, though, there have only been 37 that could be seen with the naked eye.

Multiple systems

Star systems with more than two stars are called multiple systems. Some stars that look like binaries turn out to be multiples when seen through binoculars or telescopes. The star Theta Orionis (in Orion, see page 69) can be seen through a telescope as four distinct stars, known as the Trapezium.

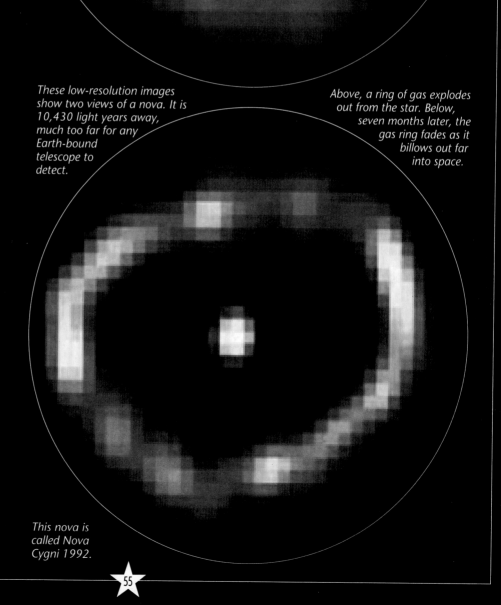

These low-resolution images show two views of a nova. It is 10,430 light years away, much too far for any Earth-bound telescope to detect.

Above, a ring of gas explodes out from the star. Below, seven months later, the gas ring fades as it billows out far into space.

This nova is called Nova Cygni 1992.

STAR PATTERNS

Since the earliest civilizations, people have noticed patterns of bright stars in the sky. These patterns are called constellations. At first glance, you may only see what looks like a jumble of twinkling stars. But with practice you can pick out the shapes of constellations.

The seven stars which form the tail and hips make the Big Dipper, a mini-pattern within Ursa Major.

Ursa Major, or the Great Bear. Here, the imaginary shape of a bear is drawn around the constellation.

Groups of stars

There are 88 constellations. Maps of all of them are shown on pages 62-75 of this book.

Dividing the stars into constellations helps to find and identify different stars in the night sky. Many constellations were named after characters or objects taken from ancient Greek myths.

Within constellations, there are smaller patterns, called asterisms. The Big Dipper is a famous asterism. It is part of the constellation Ursa Major (see top picture).

Huge distances

The constellations are made up of the most prominent stars in the sky.

From Earth, the stars in each constellation may look fairly close to one another. In reality, they are extremely far apart.

The stars in the constellation Orion, for example, vary between less than 500 light years and over 2,000 light years away from Earth. They simply look like a connected group to us because the stars lie in the same direction.

Pointers

Stars in certain constellations form pointers to other constellations in the sky.

For instance, if you imagine a line running through the two end stars of the Big Dipper in Ursa Major, the line points to Polaris, the North Star. These two useful stars are known as the Pointers.

The star maps on pages 62-75 show some ways of finding constellations by first identifying other stars or groups, and using them as pointers.

This diagram shows the constellation Orion as it looks in the sky (left) and how the stars are really positioned in space (right).

The Pointers in Ursa Major line up with Polaris in the constellation Ursa Minor.

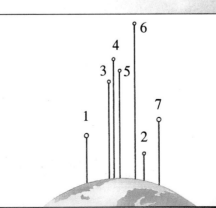

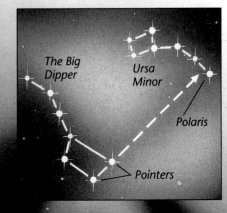

Stars on the move

Stars move through space at very high speeds, but they are so far away that any motion is impossible to detect, except with very powerful equipment. This is why constellations seem to be fixed in the sky.

100,000 years ago, the stars of the Big Dipper were shaped like this.

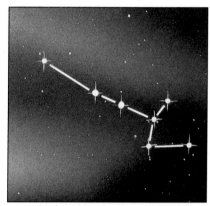

The stars of the Big Dipper today.

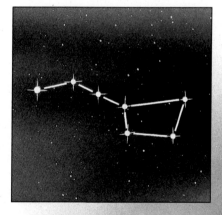

In another 100,000 years, the shape will have altered greatly.

Naming the stars

Many of the most brilliant stars have both a Greek name and an English name. The brightest star is called Sirius, a name of Greek origin. Its English name is the Dog Star.

All in Greek

Stars are also known by the name of their constellation, plus a Greek letter. Usually, the brightest star in a constellation is given the first letter of the Greek alphabet, alpha (α). The next brightest is given the second letter, beta (β), and so on. There are only 24 letters in the Greek alphabet, so if a constellation has more than 24 stars, the rest are numbered.

GREEK SYMBOLS AND THEIR NAMES

α	alpha	ν	nu
β	beta	ξ	xi
γ	gamma	o	omicron
δ	delta	π	pi
ε	epsilon	ρ	rho
ζ	zeta	σ	sigma
η	eta	τ	tau
θ	theta	υ	upsilon
ι	iota	φ	phi
κ	kappa	χ	chi
λ	lambda	ψ	psi
μ	mu	ω	omega

The five main stars of the constellation Cassiopeia. These stars give it its W-shape, which is easy to recognize.

ε

δ

γ

β

α

DESCRIBING STARS

Star brightness

Star brightness is measured on a scale called magnitude (mag. for short). The actual brilliance of a star in space is called its absolute magnitude. The brightest stars are 0 or even minus magnitude.

★ ★ ★ ★ ★ ★ ★ ★ ★ ★ ★
-1　0　1　2　3　4　5　6　7　8　9

Brightest stars　　　　　　　*Dimmest stars*

Each step on this scale indicates an increase in brightness of two and a half times.

From Earth, a very bright but distant star can appear dimmer than a less bright star that is closer to us. A star's brightness when seen from Earth is called its apparent magnitude.

Star colors

Stars are classified by their color. The hottest stars are blue or white, and the coolest are red.

Each class of star is called a spectral type, and is identified by a letter. The main spectral types are shown in the chart.

Double stars

There are two types of double stars. The first, called binary or physical double stars, orbit each other and are held together by gravity. It is difficult to tell the stars apart without a powerful telescope.

The second type, optical double stars, seem to be close together because they are in the same line of sight from Earth. In fact, they might be far apart. You can see some with the naked eye.

Earth　　　*Optical double star*

Numbers

Almost all galaxies, nebulae, star clusters and other features have an identifying number beginning with M or NGC.

M numbers refer to a catalog made in the eighteenth century by a French astronomer named Charles Messier. NGC numbers refer to the New General Catalogue, drawn up by J. L. E. Dreyer in 1888.

Some features begin with IC. This stands for Index Catalogue, which was Dreyer's list of even fainter objects, drawn up in 1908.

SPECTRAL TYPE

O
B
A
F
G
K
M

COLOR

Blue
Bluish white
White
Yellowish white
Yellow
Orange
Red

EXAMPLES

Zeta Orionis
Spica Achernar
Altair Sirius
Canopus Procyon
Sun Capella
Aldebaran Pollux
Arcturus Antares

TEMPERATURE

35,000°C　63,032°F
10,000°C　37,832°F
10,000°C　18,032°F
7,500°C　13,532°F
6,000°C　10,832°F
4,700°C　8,492°F
3,300°C　5,972°F

CONSTELLATIONS

The constellation of Crux. The four main stars form the pattern of the Southern Cross.

MAPS OF THE STARS

These star maps will help you to identify constellations in the night sky. The best time to use the maps is around 11pm.

Spotting some of the constellations can be difficult at any time, though. It's much easier from a dark place on a dark, clear night.

Map for northern hemisphere

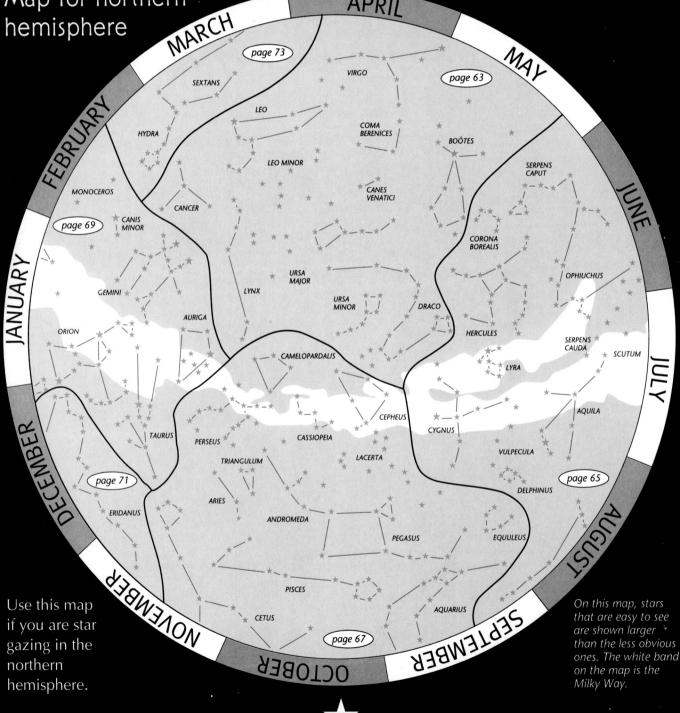

MARCH
APRIL
MAY
FEBRUARY
JUNE
JANUARY
JULY
DECEMBER
AUGUST
NOVEMBER
SEPTEMBER
OCTOBER

page 73
page 63
page 69
page 65
page 71
page 67

SEXTANS
VIRGO
LEO
COMA BERENICES
BOÖTES
HYDRA
SERPENS CAPUT
LEO MINOR
MONOCEROS
CANES VENATICI
CANCER
CANIS MINOR
CORONA BOREALIS
GEMINI
URSA MAJOR
OPHIUCHUS
LYNX
URSA MINOR
DRACO
ORION
AURIGA
HERCULES
SERPENS CAUDA
SCUTUM
CAMELOPARDALIS
LYRA
TAURUS
CEPHEUS
AQUILA
PERSEUS
CASSIOPEIA
CYGNUS
TRIANGULUM
LACERTA
VULPECULA
ARIES
DELPHINUS
ERIDANUS
ANDROMEDA
EQUULEUS
PEGASUS
PISCES
AQUARIUS
CETUS

Use this map if you are star gazing in the northern hemisphere.

On this map, stars that are easy to see are shown larger than the less obvious ones. The white band on the map is the Milky Way.

Using the maps

Find the current month in the margin around the edge. Then turn the book around until that month is nearest to you. Face south if you are in the northern hemisphere, and north if you are in the southern hemisphere. The stars in the middle and lower part of the map should be visible in the sky.

Once you know which constellations to look for, you can turn to the larger-scale maps on the following pages. These maps show which constellations are the easiest to make out. Then you can look for the others close by. The page numbers to look up are marked in each section of the maps below.

Map for southern hemisphere

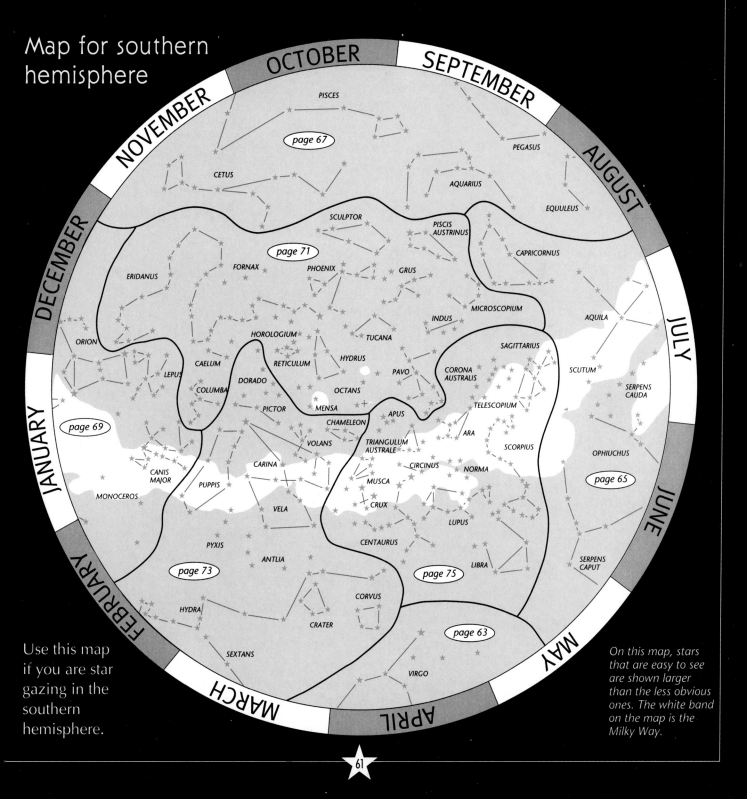

Use this map if you are star gazing in the southern hemisphere.

On this map, stars that are easy to see are shown larger than the less obvious ones. The white band on the map is the Milky Way.

DRACO TO CANCER

Draco
(the Dragon)

Draco consists of a straggling line of faint stars. The dragon's head is a group of four stars near to Vega, the fifth brightest star in the sky. The tail loops around Ursa Minor.

Canes Venatici
(the Hunting Dogs)

The hunting dogs chase the Great Bear (Ursa Major) and the Little Bear (Ursa Minor) through the sky. Bear hunting was a popular sport in the seventeenth century, when this constellation was named.

Boötes
(the Herdsman)

Try finding Boötes by using the tail of Ursa Major as a pointer. Arcturus, at the base of Boötes, is the fourth brightest star in the sky.

From January 1-6 each year, there is a meteor shower, called the Quadrantids, in the area around Boötes and the tail of Ursa Major. This is not easily visible until after midnight.

Coma Berenices
(Berenice's Hair)

According to a Greek myth, Berenice cut off all her beautiful hair, which the god Jupiter then placed among the stars. The three main stars in the constellation are shown on the map, although it may be difficult to pick them out from other stars.

On a dark night, you can see the Coma cluster, an open star cluster, with the naked eye.

Virgo
(the Virgin)

This constellation represents the goddess of fertility and harvest. Virgo's brightest star is Spica, which means "ear of corn". Spica is 220 light years away from Earth.

Ursa Minor
(the Little Bear)

This constellation's brightest star is Polaris, the pole star. It is the only star in the sky which appears not to move. This is because it is in line with the Earth's axis, directly above the north pole. As the Earth rotates, Polaris stays in the same place relative to it, but other stars appear to move across the sky, around Polaris.

Once you have found Polaris, line it up with a landmark so you can find it again from the same place. It shows which direction is north.

Ursa Major
(the Great Bear)

The seven brightest stars in this constellation make an asterism called the Big Dipper, Plow or Saucepan. The stars Dubhe and Merak in the Big Dipper are called the Pointers. An imaginary line through them points to Polaris, the pole star.

Lynx

This constellation was given its name because only people with good eyesight, like a lynx, can see it. It is a line of faint stars.

Leo Minor
(the Small Lion)

This constellation is very faint and difficult to spot.

Cancer
(the Crab)

These are faint stars between Leo and Gemini (shown on page 69). Cancer contains the spectacular M44 open star cluster, called the Beehive or Praesepe.

Leo
(the Lion)

Leo is one of the few constellations which looks like the thing it is named after – a crouching lion. The head region is sometimes known as the Sickle or Backward Question Mark.

Around November 17 each year, a meteor shower, called the Leonids, occurs near the head of Leo. This is not easily visible until after midnight.

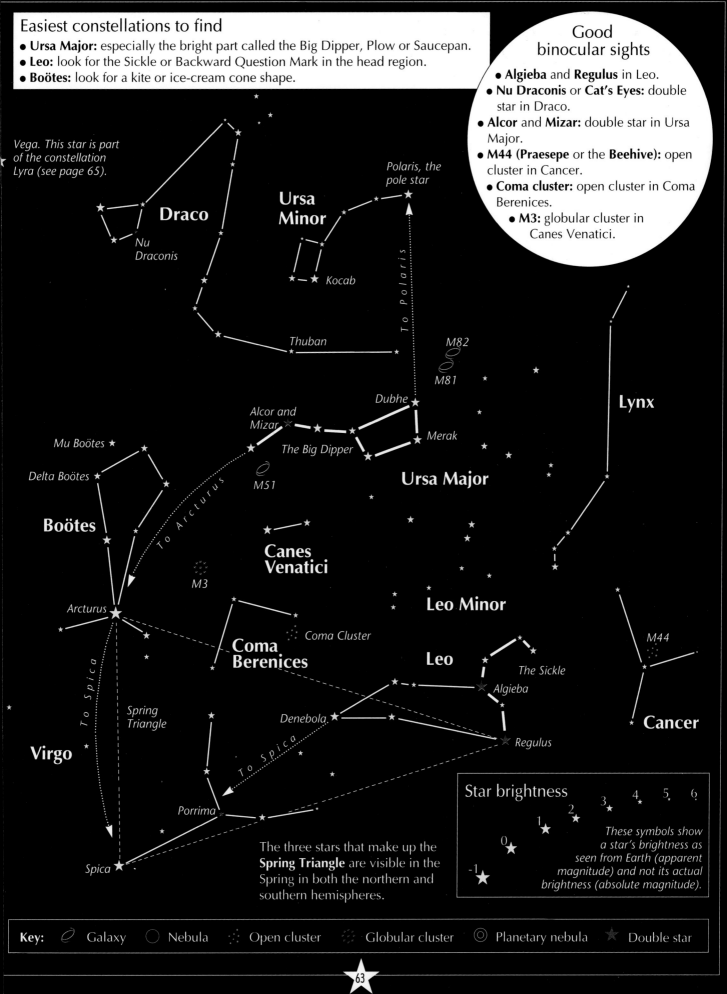

Easiest constellations to find

- **Ursa Major:** especially the bright part called the Big Dipper, Plow or Saucepan.
- **Leo:** look for the Sickle or Backward Question Mark in the head region.
- **Boötes:** look for a kite or ice-cream cone shape.

Good binocular sights

- **Algieba** and **Regulus** in Leo.
- **Nu Draconis** or **Cat's Eyes:** double star in Draco.
- **Alcor** and **Mizar:** double star in Ursa Major.
- **M44 (Praesepe** or the **Beehive):** open cluster in Cancer.
- **Coma cluster:** open cluster in Coma Berenices.
- **M3:** globular cluster in Canes Venatici.

Vega. This star is part of the constellation Lyra (see page 65).

Draco

Nu Draconis

Polaris, the pole star

Ursa Minor

Kocab

To Polaris

Thuban

M82

M81

Lynx

Dubhe

Alcor and Mizar

The Big Dipper

Merak

Ursa Major

Mu Boötes

To Arcturus

M51

Delta Boötes

Boötes

Canes Venatici

M3

Leo Minor

Coma Cluster

Arcturus

Coma Berenices

Leo

M44

The Sickle

Algieba

Cancer

To Spica

Spring Triangle

Denebola

Regulus

Virgo

To Spica

Porrima

Spica

The three stars that make up the **Spring Triangle** are visible in the Spring in both the northern and southern hemispheres.

Star brightness

1 2 3 4 5 6

0

-1

These symbols show a star's brightness as seen from Earth (apparent magnitude) and not its actual brightness (absolute magnitude).

Key: ⊘ Galaxy ○ Nebula ⠿ Open cluster ⠿ Globular cluster ◎ Planetary nebula ★ Double star

CYGNUS TO SERPENS

Cygnus
(the Swan)
Cygnus contains a cross shape, called the Northern Cross asterism. It has the bright star Deneb at the top and Albireo at the bottom.

Deneb is one of the brightest known stars in the galaxy. It is over 60,000 times more luminous than the Sun. It forms one corner of the Summer Triangle.

Delphinus
(the Dolphin)
Delphinus is compact, with a distinctive shape. The star Epsilon Delphini is 950 light years away, much farther away than the other stars in this constellation.

Sagitta
(the Arrow)
Sagitta* consists of four faint stars in an arrow shape.

Capricornus
(the Sea Goat)
Some astronomers refer to Capricornus as the smile in the sky. It is a distorted triangle of faint stars.

At one end is the double star, Alpha Capricorni. This consists of the stars, Alpha 1 and Alpha 2. Alpha 2 is also known as Algedi or Giedi. You can just see both stars with the naked eye.

Aquila
(the Eagle)
The bright star Altair in Aquila forms part of the Summer Triangle. Altair is the eleventh brightest star in the sky and it is flanked by two fainter stars.

Scutum
(the Shield)
Scutum is faint, but just visible with the naked eye. Look for M11, the Wild Duck open cluster in Scutum, near the base of Aquila.

Vulpecula
(the Fox)
Vulpecula contains M27, a planetary nebula called the Dumbbell Nebula. In 1967, the first pulsar was discovered in Vulpecula, although this is too dim to see.

Lyra
(the Lyre)
Small but easy to spot, Lyra's brightest star is Vega, the fifth brightest in the sky.

Ophiuchus
(the Serpent Bearer)
Ophiuchus is a very large group of stars. Ophiuchus is holding a snake, the constellation Serpens, so the two constellations are joined.

Hercules
This constellation is named after a Greek hero. The middle of Hercules looks like a slightly distorted square. This is called the Keystone. M13, one of the best globular clusters in the sky, lies on its right-hand side.

Corona Borealis
(the Northern Crown)
This is a semicircle of faint stars between Vega and Arcturus (in the constellation Boötes, see page 63).

Corona Borealis contains a recurring nova, known as the Blaze Star. This last brightened in February 1946 to apparent magnitude 2.3 from its normal magnitude 10. It will not be visible until it brightens again.

Serpens
(the Serpent)
Serpens is the only constellation formed of two separate parts: Caput (the head) and Cauda (the tail). They lie on either side of Ophiuchus.

In Serpens Cauda is the nebula M16 (the Eagle or Star Queen Nebula). It has an eagle-shaped dust and gas cloud in its middle.

You need a fairly large telescope to see M16 in any detail. Hubble Space Telescope images have revealed stunning areas of star birth within it.

*Sagitta is very faint, and is not shown on this map

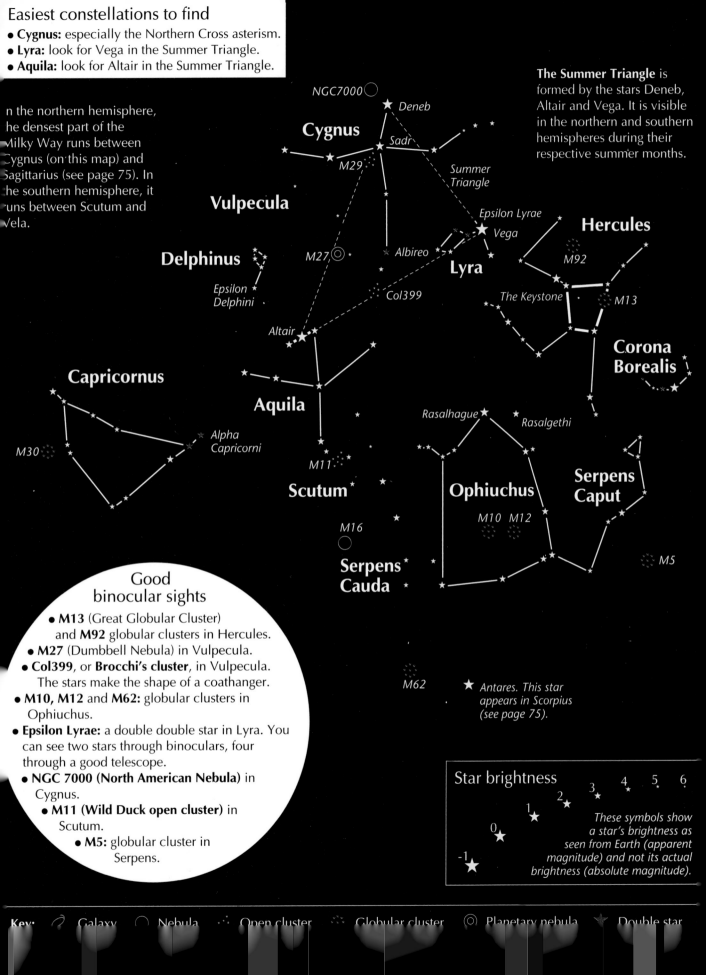

Easiest constellations to find

- **Cygnus:** especially the Northern Cross asterism.
- **Lyra:** look for Vega in the Summer Triangle.
- **Aquila:** look for Altair in the Summer Triangle.

n the northern hemisphere, he densest part of the Milky Way runs between Cygnus (on this map) and Sagittarius (see page 75). In he southern hemisphere, it runs between Scutum and Vela.

The Summer Triangle is formed by the stars Deneb, Altair and Vega. It is visible in the northern and southern hemispheres during their respective summer months.

NGC7000

Deneb

Cygnus

Sadr

M29

Summer Triangle

Vulpecula

Epsilon Lyrae

Vega

Hercules

Delphinus

M27

Albireo

Lyra

M92

Epsilon Delphini

Col399

The Keystone

M13

Altair

Capricornus

Aquila

Rasalhague

Rasalgethi

Corona Borealis

M30

Alpha Capricorni

M11

Scutum

M16

Ophiuchus

M10 M12

Serpens Caput

M5

Serpens Cauda

M62

Good binocular sights

- **M13** (Great Globular Cluster) and **M92** globular clusters in Hercules.
- **M27** (Dumbbell Nebula) in Vulpecula.
- **Col399**, or **Brocchi's cluster**, in Vulpecula. The stars make the shape of a coathanger.
- **M10, M12** and **M62:** globular clusters in Ophiuchus.
- **Epsilon Lyrae:** a double double star in Lyra. You can see two stars through binoculars, four through a good telescope.
- **NGC 7000 (North American Nebula)** in Cygnus.
- **M11 (Wild Duck open cluster)** in Scutum.
- **M5:** globular cluster in Serpens.

★ *Antares. This star appears in Scorpius (see page 75).*

Star brightness

4   5   6

3 ★

2 ★

1 ★

0 ★

-1 ★

These symbols show a star's brightness as seen from Earth (apparent magnitude) and not its actual brightness (absolute magnitude).

Key: ⊘ Galaxy   ◯ Nebula   ⸭ Open cluster   ⸬ Globular cluster   ◎ Planetary nebula   ★ Double star

CAMELOPARDALIS TO AQUARIUS

Camelopardalis (the Giraffe)
It isn't easy to see any of these stars with the naked eye.

Perseus
Perseus was a Greek hero. There are many open star clusters within Perseus but the showpiece is the double cluster of NGC869 and 884.

The eclipsing variable binary star Algol has a period of nearly three days. As one star passes in front of the other, Algol fades to about half its usual brightness.

A meteor shower occurs in Perseus between July 25 and August 20 every year, peaking on August 12.

Andromeda
Andromeda was a princess who was rescued from a monster by Perseus.

Andromeda contains M31, the Andromeda or Great Spiral Galaxy. At 2.9 million light years away, it is the farthest object visible to the naked eye.

Triangulum (the Triangle)
The Triangle is a compact pattern made up of three stars. It is fairly easy to spot on a dark night. It contains M33, the Pinwheel Galaxy.

Aries (the Ram)
Aries is made up of four main stars.

Pisces (the Fishes)
In Greek myth, these were two fishes tied by a long ribbon. The constellation is not easy to find. The most visible part is the circlet under the Square of Pegasus, known as the Western Fish, or Circlet.

Cetus (the Whale)
Cetus contains the variable star Mira. For half the year, Mira is visible to the naked eye. Then it fades to invisibility. It has a period of 331 days.

Cepheus
Cepheus looks a little like the side of a house. In Greek myth, Cepheus was the King of Ethiopia, and married to Cassiopeia (see below). The brightest star is Alderamin.

Delta Cephei is a variable star with a period of 5 days, 8 hours and 48 minutes.

Cassiopeia
Cassiopeia sits side by side with her husband Cepheus. The W-shape* is easy to spot. Two of its end stars can be used as pointers to the constellation Andromeda.

Lacerta (the Lizard)
Lacerta is a zig-zag of faint stars, which is hard to find.

Pegasus
Pegasus was a flying horse in Greek mythology. Three of its stars plus the end star of Andromeda make up the Square of Pegasus. This is fairly easy to spot, as it is one of the largest geometrical shapes in the night sky.

Equuleus (the Foal)
Equuleus is hard to find, even on a clear night. The two stars that form Delta Equuleus, a double star, are extremely close in outer space terms. Even so, they are as far apart as the Sun and Jupiter.

Aquarius (the Water Bearer)
Aquarius isn't easy to find. The small group of stars near the top represents a water jar. The stars below show a stream of water.

Aquarius contains a planetary nebula, Helix, which can be seen through binoculars on a very dark night as a dim blur about half the size of the Moon. It is fairly hard to spot.

From April 24 to May 20, a meteor-shower, called Eta Aquarids, appears in this area.

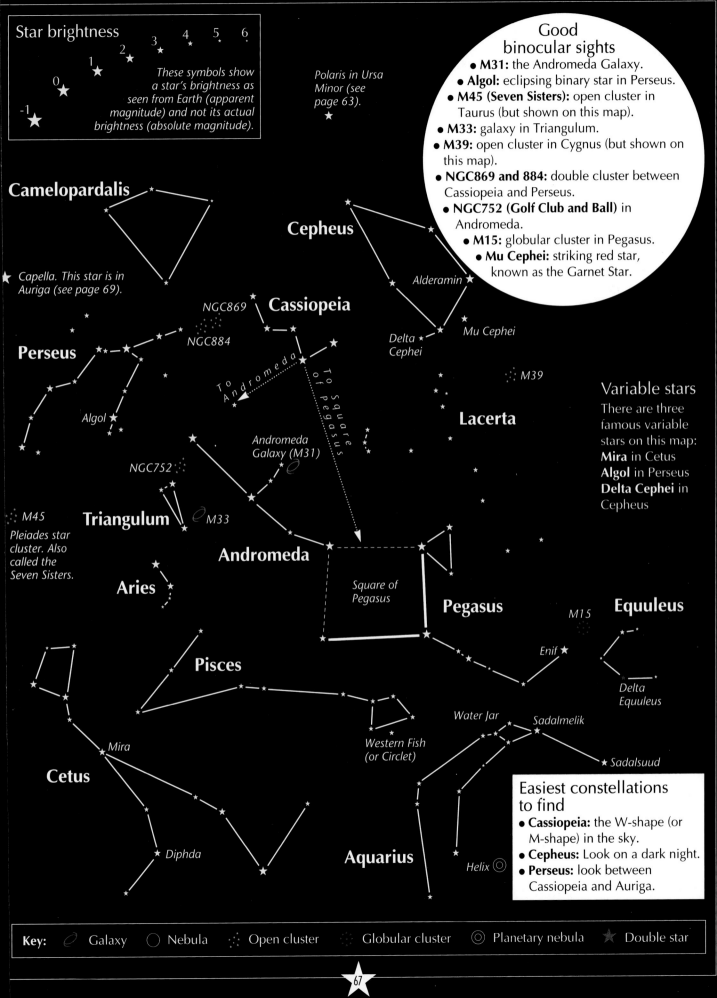

Star brightness

0   1   2   3   4   5   6

These symbols show a star's brightness as seen from Earth (apparent magnitude) and not its actual brightness (absolute magnitude).

-1

Polaris in Ursa Minor (see page 63).

Polaris in Ursa Minor (see page 63).

Good binocular sights

- **M31:** the Andromeda Galaxy.
- **Algol:** eclipsing binary star in Perseus.
- **M45 (Seven Sisters):** open cluster in Taurus (but shown on this map).
- **M33:** galaxy in Triangulum.
- **M39:** open cluster in Cygnus (but shown on this map).
- **NGC869 and 884:** double cluster between Cassiopeia and Perseus.
- **NGC752 (Golf Club and Ball)** in Andromeda.
- **M15:** globular cluster in Pegasus.
- **Mu Cephei:** striking red star, known as the Garnet Star.

Camelopardalis

Capella. *This star is in Auriga (see page 69).*

Capella. This star is in Auriga (see page 69).

Cepheus

Cassiopeia

NGC869

NGC884

Perseus

Algol

To Andromeda

To Square of Pegasus

Alderamin

Delta Cephei

Mu Cephei

M39

Lacerta

Variable stars

There are three famous variable stars on this map:
Mira in Cetus
Algol in Perseus
Delta Cephei in Cepheus

NGC752

Andromeda Galaxy (M31)

Triangulum

M33

Andromeda

M45
Pleiades star cluster. Also called the Seven Sisters.

Aries

Pisces

Square of Pegasus

Pegasus

M15

Equuleus

Enif

Delta Equuleus

Mira

Cetus

Diphda

Western Fish (or Circlet)

Water Jar

Sadalmelik

Sadalsuud

Aquarius

Helix

Easiest constellations to find

- **Cassiopeia:** the W-shape (or M-shape) in the sky.
- **Cepheus:** Look on a dark night.
- **Perseus:** look between Cassiopeia and Auriga.

Key: ⊘ Galaxy   ◯ Nebula   ⠒ Open cluster   ⣿ Globular cluster   ◎ Planetary nebula   ★ Double star

GEMINI TO LEPUS

Gemini
(the Twins)

The stars Castor and Pollux in Gemini are often referred to as the Twins. Castor is actually six stars close together, but you cannot see them separately, even through binoculars.

From December 7-15 every year there is a meteor shower, called the Geminids, in this area of the sky.

Canis Minor
(the Small Dog)

This constellation represents the smaller of the two dogs that belonged to Orion, the mythical Greek hunter.

Procyon in Canis Minor is the eighth brightest star in the sky – and at only 11 light years from Earth, it is one of the closest.

There are lots of star clusters in the sky around Canis Minor, Monoceros and Canis Major (see below).

Monoceros
(the Unicorn)

Monoceros is hard to see. Look along it using binoculars and you should be able to see the many, faint open star clusters that reside there. In the northern hemisphere's winter, this is the brightest part of the Milky Way.

Canis Major
(the Great Dog)

This is a compact group of bright stars. Sirius (the Dog Star) is the brightest star in the sky. It is about 8.6 light years away from Earth. There is an open star cluster, called M41, in Canis Major.

Auriga
(the Charioteer)

This constellation is shaped like a kite. A distinct but faint triangle, known as the Kids, is nearby. The variable star Epsilon Aurigae is one of the Kids. Every 27 years, it is eclipsed by a mysterious dark companion, possibly a huge disk of gas and dust.

Capella, the sixth brightest star in the sky, is 42 light years away. It is in fact six stars but even with a powerful telescope you can only see one. The star clusters M36, M37 and M38 are nearby.

Taurus
(the Bull)

The group of stars that make up the bull's head is known as the Hyades. The bull's eye is the double star Aldebaran.

The Pleiades star cluster is also in Taurus. This is often known as the Seven Sisters, although most people can only see six stars with the naked eye. According to

Greek legend, the Pleiades were sisters placed in the sky to protect them from Orion, who was chasing them.

Taurus also contains M1, the Crab Nebula. This is the remnant of a supernova that exploded in 1054. In its middle is a pulsar, the remains of the original star. It spins 33 times per second.

From October 20 to November 30 each year there is a meteor shower, called the Taurids, in this area of the sky.

Orion

Orion was a great hunter in Greek mythology. The constellation contains many bright stars. The blue-white Rigel is the seventh brightest star in the sky. The red star Betelgeuse is a variable star with an irregular cycle.

Look for the Orion nebula just below the three stars that form Orion's belt. It contains Theta Orionis, a multiple system of four stars, also known as the Trapezium.

Around October 22 each year, there is a meteor shower, called the Orionids, in between Orion and Gemini.

Lepus
(the Hare)

The hare was the animal that Orion most liked to hunt.

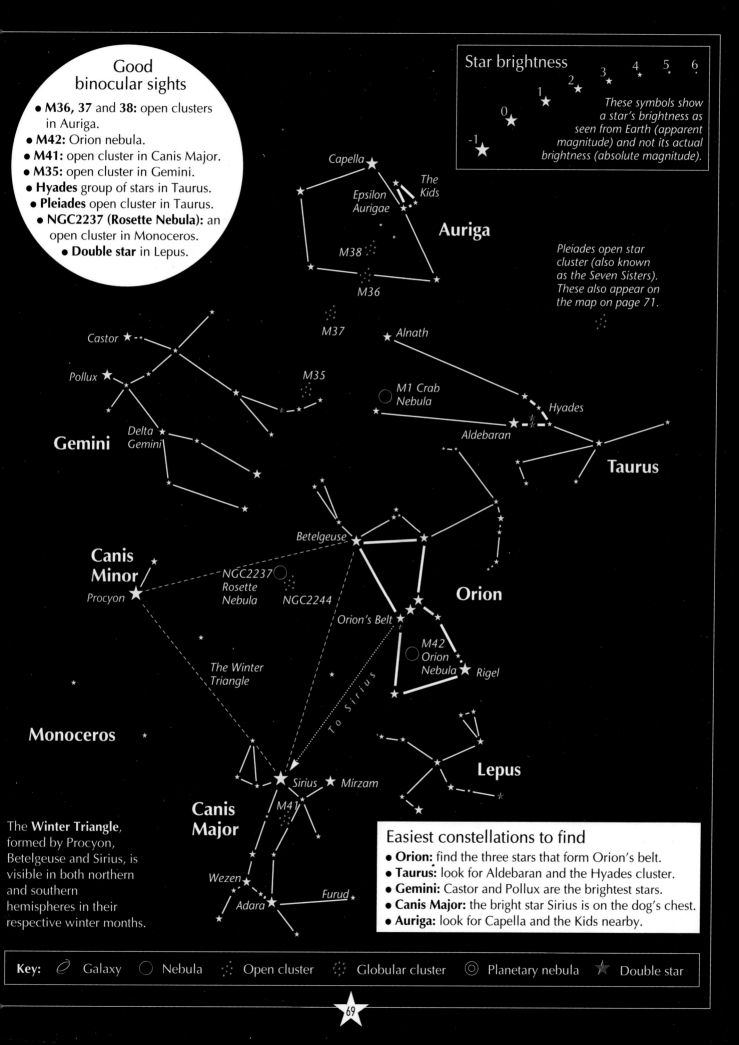

Good binocular sights

- **M36, 37 and 38:** open clusters in Auriga.
- **M42:** Orion nebula.
- **M41:** open cluster in Canis Major.
- **M35:** open cluster in Gemini.
- **Hyades** group of stars in Taurus.
- **Pleiades** open cluster in Taurus.
- **NGC2237 (Rosette Nebula):** an open cluster in Monoceros.
- **Double star** in Lepus.

Star brightness

These symbols show a star's brightness as seen from Earth (apparent magnitude) and not its actual brightness (absolute magnitude).

Pleiades open star cluster (also known as the Seven Sisters). These also appear on the map on page 71.

Capella
The Kids
Epsilon Aurigae
Auriga
M38
M36
M37
Alnath

Castor
Pollux
Gemini
Delta Gemini
M35
M1 Crab Nebula
Aldebaran
Hyades
Taurus

Betelgeuse
Canis Minor
Procyon
NGC2237 Rosette Nebula
NGC2244
Orion's Belt
Orion
M42 Orion Nebula
Rigel

The Winter Triangle

Monoceros

Canis Major
Sirius
Mirzam
M41
Wezen
Adara
Furud

Lepus

To Sirius

The **Winter Triangle**, formed by Procyon, Betelgeuse and Sirius, is visible in both northern and southern hemispheres in their respective winter months.

Easiest constellations to find

- **Orion:** find the three stars that form Orion's belt.
- **Taurus:** look for Aldebaran and the Hyades cluster.
- **Gemini:** Castor and Pollux are the brightest stars.
- **Canis Major:** the bright star Sirius is on the dog's chest.
- **Auriga:** look for Capella and the Kids nearby.

Key: ⊘ Galaxy ◯ Nebula ⁖ Open cluster ⁛ Globular cluster ◎ Planetary nebula ★ Double star

COLUMBA TO MICROSCOPIUM

Columba
(Noah's Dove)
This is a distinct group of stars lying near Canopus in Carina (see map on page 73).

Horologium
(the Pendulum Clock)
In this constellation, only the star nearest to Caelum (see below) is easily visible.

Caelum
(the Chisel)
This consists of a few very faint stars.

Reticulum
(the Net)
This is a distinct group of faint stars which lies between Canopus in Carina and Achernar in Eridanus.

Mensa
(the Table Mountain)
Only look for this faint constellation on a very clear night. It is near the Large Magellanic Cloud.

Hydrus
(the Small Water Snake)
The three brightest stars in Hydrus make a large triangle between the misty patches of the Magellanic Clouds.

Octans
(the Octant)
This surrounds the imaginary point directly above the south pole and in line with the axis of the Earth. This point,

marked with a cross on the map, is known as the south celestial pole. Unlike the north celestial pole, which is marked by Polaris (the pole star), there is no star to mark the exact south celestial pole.

Pavo
(the Peacock)
Pavo has several fairly bright stars quite close together. These help to locate it. The variable star Kappa Pavonis changes from dim to bright and back every nine days.

Indus
(the Indian)
Indus runs between Pavo, Microscopium and Grus.

Fornax
(the Furnace)
This small constellation lies next to part of the curve of Eridanus.

Eridanus
Eridanus is a long, winding line of stars named after a mythological Greek river. Epsilon Eridani is 10.8 light years away from the solar system and, in absolute magnitude, is similar to our Sun. Achernar is the ninth brightest star in the sky. It is 85 light years away.

Tucana
(the Toucan)
Tucana has the Small Magellanic Cloud within its

boundary. The star cluster 47Tuc (NGC104) is the second finest globular cluster in the sky, after Omega Centauri.

Sculptor
This consists of faint stars and is very hard to distinguish.

Phoenix
Phoenix was named after the mythological bird that rises from its own ashes.

Piscis Austrinus
(the Southern Fish)
This includes the star Fomalhaut, which is 24 light years from Earth. It may have planets of its own.

Grus
(the Crane)
The brightest star in this conspicuous group is Alnair.

Microscopium
(the Microscope)
The stars in this constellation are faint. It is extremely difficult to make out.

The Small and Large Magellanic Clouds
The Small and Large Magellanic Clouds are irregular shaped galaxies. They are satellite galaxies to our Milky Way galaxy, held close to it by its immense gravity.

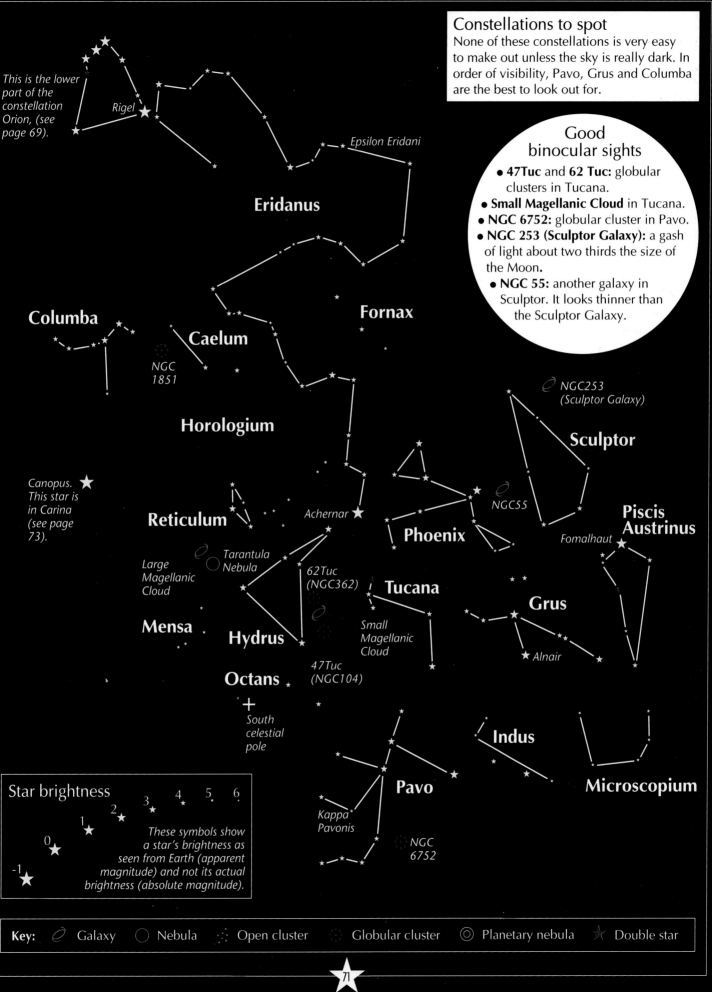

Constellations to spot

None of these constellations is very easy to make out unless the sky is really dark. In order of visibility, Pavo, Grus and Columba are the best to look out for.

Good binocular sights

- **47Tuc** and **62 Tuc**: globular clusters in Tucana.
- **Small Magellanic Cloud** in Tucana.
- **NGC 6752**: globular cluster in Pavo.
- **NGC 253 (Sculptor Galaxy):** a gash of light about two thirds the size of the Moon.
- **NGC 55**: another galaxy in Sculptor. It looks thinner than the Sculptor Galaxy.

This is the lower part of the constellation Orion, (see page 69).

Canopus. This star is in Carina (see page 73).

Star brightness

These symbols show a star's brightness as seen from Earth (apparent magnitude) and not its actual brightness (absolute magnitude).

Key: ⊘ Galaxy ◯ Nebula ⋮ Open cluster ⋰ Globular cluster ◎ Planetary nebula ✦ Double star

71

CORVUS TO DORADO

Corvus
(the Crow)
This distinct group of four main stars is in a somewhat barren area of the sky, so it is fairly easy to spot.

Crater
(the Cup)
The group of main stars in this constellation looks a little like a fainter version of Corvus.

Antlia
(the Air Pump)
This group of faint stars is very difficult to spot.

Vela
(the Sail)
Vela's outline is marked by bright stars. When you look at Vela through binoculars, you will see many smaller stars as well.

Along with Iota and Epsilon Carinae, Kappa and Delta Velorum make up the False Cross.

Chameleon
Chameleon is made of four faint stars and it cannot be seen easily, like a real chameleon disguising itself!

Volans
(the Flying Fish)
This distinct group of faint stars is partly enclosed by the constellation Carina.

Sextans
(the Sextant)
This small group of faint stars lies between Leo (see page 63) and Hydra.

Hydra
(the Water Snake)
This is the longest and largest constellation in the sky. It is a sprawling line of mainly faint stars. The head is a conspicuous group of stars.

The only bright star in this constellation is Alphard, sometimes called the "solitary one", since there are no other bright stars nearby.

Pyxis
(the Compass)
This constellation consists of just three main stars between Vela and Puppis.

Puppis
(the Stern)
Lots of stars and open clusters are visible through binoculars in this area.

Carina
(the Keel)
At one end is Canopus, which is 1,200 light years away and is the second brightest star in the night sky. Along with two stars in Vela, Epsilon and Iota Carinae make up the False Cross.

Pictor
(the Easel)
Pictures of Beta Pictoris have shown a circle of material surrounding the star. Many astronomers think this is evidence of planets forming, though none have been seen.

Dorado
(the Swordfish)
Dorado includes the irregular galaxy known as the Large Magellanic Cloud. It is only visible from the southern hemisphere. It looks like a misty patch.

A famous supernova took place in the Large Magellanic Cloud in 1987. It was easily the brightest, and closest, supernova since 1604.

A bright nebula, called Tarantula, can be seen in the Large Magellanic Cloud.

Argo Navis
(the ship)
In ancient times, Vela, Puppis and Carina were part of one huge constellation called Argo Navis. The astronomer Nicolas Lacaille split them up into separate constellations in 1756. The Milky Way runs the entire length of Argo Navis, culminating in brilliant star clouds around the Carinae Nebula (NGC3372).

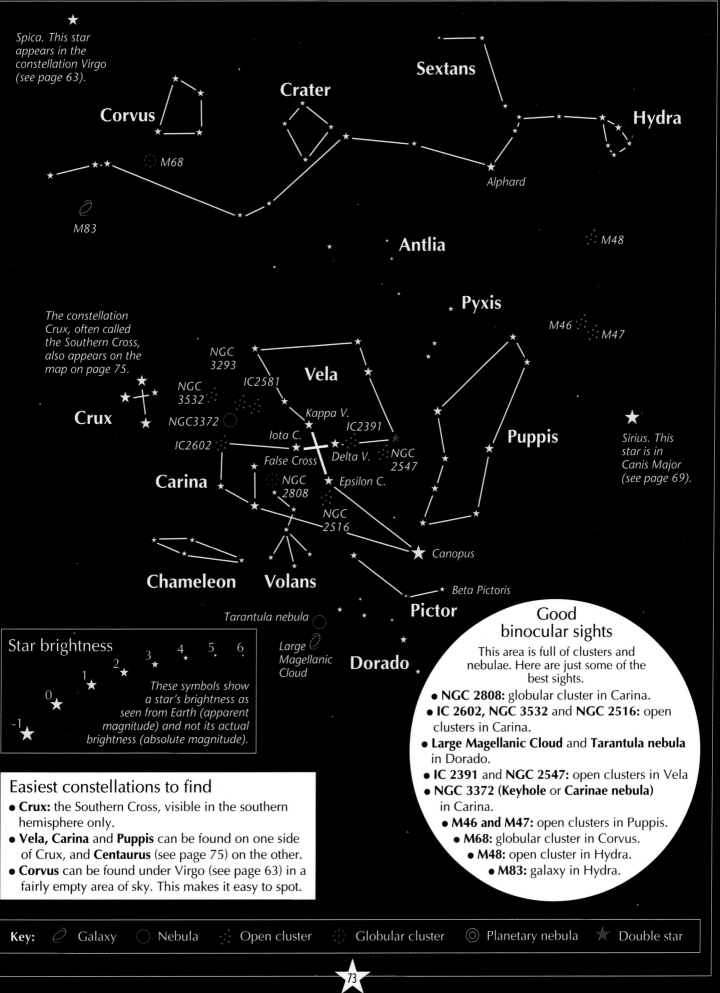

Spica. This star appears in the constellation Virgo (see page 63).

Corvus

Crater

Sextans

Hydra

M68

Alphard

M83

Antlia

M48

Pyxis

M46

M47

The constellation Crux, often called the Southern Cross, also appears on the map on page 75.

NGC 3293

IC2581

Vela

NGC 3532

NGC3372

Kappa V.

IC2391

Crux

Iota C.

Delta V.

Puppis

IC2602

False Cross

NGC 2547

Carina

NGC 2808

Epsilon C.

Sirius. This star is in Canis Major (see page 69).

NGC 2516

Canopus

Chameleon

Volans

Beta Pictoris

Pictor

Tarantula nebula

Large Magellanic Cloud

Dorado

Star brightness

3   4   5   6

2

1

0

-1

These symbols show a star's brightness as seen from Earth (apparent magnitude) and not its actual brightness (absolute magnitude).

Good binocular sights

This area is full of clusters and nebulae. Here are just some of the best sights.

- **NGC 2808:** globular cluster in Carina.
- **IC 2602, NGC 3532** and **NGC 2516:** open clusters in Carina.
- **Large Magellanic Cloud** and **Tarantula nebula** in Dorado.
- **IC 2391** and **NGC 2547:** open clusters in Vela
- **NGC 3372 (Keyhole** or **Carinae nebula)** in Carina.
- **M46** and **M47:** open clusters in Puppis.
- **M68:** globular cluster in Corvus.
- **M48:** open cluster in Hydra.
- **M83:** galaxy in Hydra.

Easiest constellations to find

- **Crux:** the Southern Cross, visible in the southern hemisphere only.
- **Vela, Carina** and **Puppis** can be found on one side of Crux, and **Centaurus** (see page 75) on the other.
- **Corvus** can be found under Virgo (see page 63) in a fairly empty area of sky. This makes it easy to spot.

Key: ⬭ Galaxy   ◯ Nebula   ⣿ Open cluster   ⣿ Globular cluster   ◎ Planetary nebula   ★ Double star

SAGITTARIUS TO CRUX

Sagittarius
(the Archer)
Sagittarius is sometimes called the Teapot. It has many bright stars. Above the "spout" is the M8 nebula, where new stars are forming. Other nebulae are visible with binoculars.

Corona Australis
(the Southern Crown)
The faint stars of Corona Australis make a curve.

Telescopium
(the Telescope)
This group of faint stars is near the tail of the large constellation Scorpius.

Ara
(the Altar)
You might find Ara by looking between the bright star Alpha Centauri (in Centaurus) and the tail of Scorpius.

NGC6397, our closest globular cluster, lies in this constellation. It is 8,400 light years away.

Circinus
(the Compass)
This consists of three faint stars near to the bright star Alpha Centauri in Centaurus.

Triangulum Australe
(the Southern Triangle)
This constellation was first identified by the Italian explorer Amerigo Vespucci, in 1503. (He is more famous for establishing that America is not part of Asia as earlier explorers had thought.)

Apus
(the Bird of Paradise)
Apus is an inconspicuous group of faint stars.

Musca
(the Fly)
This faint constellation is next to Crux, the Southern Cross.

Scorpius
(the Scorpion)
Scorpius is mostly made of bright stars, which form a fairly convincing scorpion shape. Antares is a very bright red star.

With binoculars, you can see many faint open and globular star clusters.

Libra
(the Scales)
Four faint stars form the main part of Libra.

Alpha Librae is a double star. Beta Librae is the only star that appears green to the naked eye.

Lupus
(the Wolf)
Lupus is a distinctive pattern of bright stars, stretching between Alpha Centauri and Antares in Scorpius.

Norma
(the Level)
This is a group of very faint stars. The region is, however, filled with star clusters because Norma lies in the direction of the thickest part of the Milky Way that we see in the night sky.

Centaurus
(the Centaur)
A centaur is a mythical creature, half-man, half-horse.

Alpha Centauri is the third brightest star in the sky. After the Sun, it is the second closest star to us, 4.3 light years away. It is only visible in the southern hemisphere.

The faint Proxima Centauri (visible with a telescope) is Alpha Centauri's companion. It is the closest star to the Earth, 4.25 light years away.

Omega Centauri is the most visible globular cluster in the night sky. It has one million stars and is one of the closest globular clusters to us.

Crux
(the Southern Cross)
This is perhaps the most famous constellation in the southern hemisphere.

Alpha and Gamma Crucis point to the south celestial pole (the point directly above the south pole on Earth).

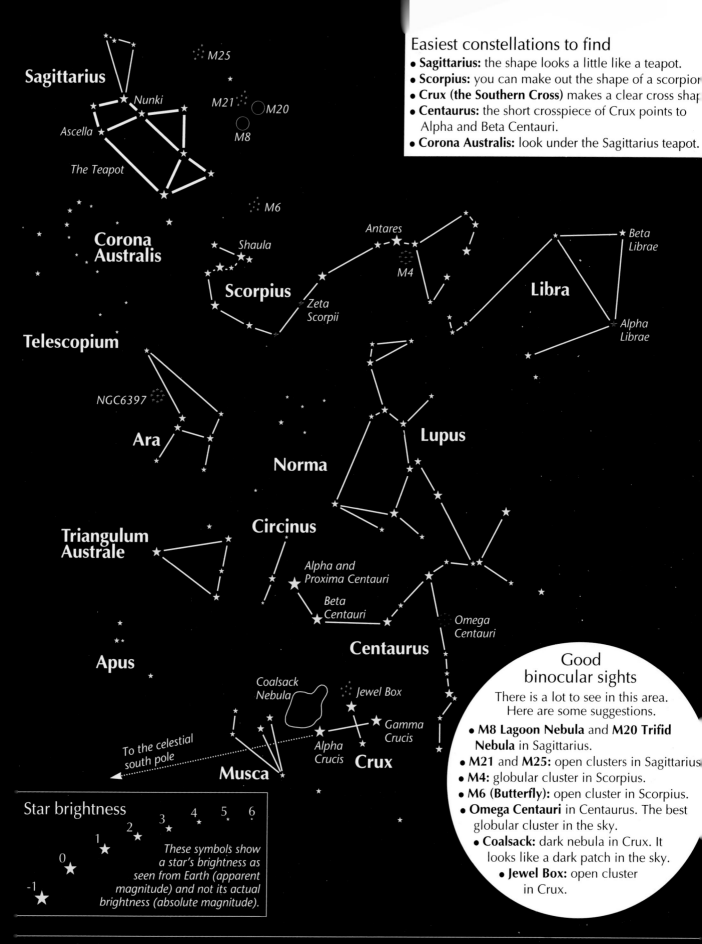

Sagittarius

M25

Nunki

M21   ○*M20*

Ascella

○ *M8*

The Teapot

Corona Australis

M6

Telescopium

NGC6397

Ara

Triangulum Australe

Circinus

Shaula

Scorpius

Zeta Scorpii

Antares

M4

Lupus

Norma

Alpha and Proxima Centauri

Beta Centauri

Centaurus

Omega Centauri

Apus

Coalsack Nebula

Jewel Box

To the celestial south pole

Musca

Alpha Crucis

Gamma Crucis

Crux

Libra

★ *Beta Librae*

Alpha Librae

Easiest constellations to find

- **Sagittarius:** the shape looks a little like a teapot.
- **Scorpius:** you can make out the shape of a scorpion
- **Crux (the Southern Cross)** makes a clear cross shar
- **Centaurus:** the short crosspiece of Crux points to Alpha and Beta Centauri.
- **Corona Australis:** look under the Sagittarius teapot.

Good binocular sights

There is a lot to see in this area. Here are some suggestions.

- **M8 Lagoon Nebula** and **M20 Trifid Nebula** in Sagittarius.
- **M21** and **M25:** open clusters in Sagittarius
- **M4:** globular cluster in Scorpius.
- **M6 (Butterfly):** open cluster in Scorpius.
- **Omega Centauri** in Centaurus. The best globular cluster in the sky.
- **Coalsack:** dark nebula in Crux. It looks like a dark patch in the sky.
- **Jewel Box:** open cluster in Crux.

Star brightness

0   1   2   3   4   5   6

-1

These symbols show a star's brightness as seen from Earth (apparent magnitude) and not its actual brightness (absolute magnitude).

Key: ⬭ Galaxy   ○ Nebula   ∴ Open cluster   Globular cluster   ◎ Planetary nebula   ★ Double star

HOME ASTRONOMY

I f you would like to identify and observe stars and planets yourself, there are several pieces of equipment that you will find very useful. Here are some suggestions for what you might need.

Focusing controls

Lightweight binoculars

Eyepiece

Front lenses. The technical name for these is "objective lenses"

The lens's diameter is the measurement across the lens from one side to the other.

Star maps

The star maps that appear in this book on pages 60-75 will help you to find your way around the night sky, and get to know the different constellations.

Star maps help you to find your way around the night sky.

Planispheres

Planispheres are movable maps of the night skies. They can be moved around to show which stars can be seen at any time. Planispheres are made to be used in particular parts of the world, so make sure you buy one that's correct for your part.

Binoculars

Binoculars are made in different sizes and powers. These are indicated by a pair of numbers, such as 7 x 35, 10 x 50 or 20 x 80. The first number tells you by how many times the binoculars will magnify an object. The second number is the diameter, in millimeters, of each front lens.

Using binoculars

Big, powerful binoculars will show you more than smaller ones. But big binoculars are heavy and will become hard to hold still.

For this reason, it is best to use binoculars that you find comfortable. Try out different pairs, and don't buy any that feel too heavy. Good sizes to try are 7 x 35 or 10 x 50.

If you do use large or heavy binoculars, it is best to mount them on a tripod. This will keep them steady while you observe the sky.

Telescopes

Good telescopes are expensive. The cheaper versions are not very good and few astronomers recommend them. For the cost of a cheap telescope, it is better to buy a very good pair of binoculars.

You can buy telescopes second-hand. Look for advertisements in astronomy magazines and seek the advice of an experienced astronomer before you buy.

What can you see?

With binoculars, you can see a bigger area of the sky. With a good telescope, you can see more detail.

Stars seen with naked eye.

Same stars seen through binoculars.

Same stars seen through a good telescope.

There is a short guide to telescopes on page 80. The telescope below is a refractor telescope. It uses a lens to collect light.

Finder scope. This small telescope helps you line up the main telescope.

Eyepiece

Your telescope will need a mount. Without one, you will not be able to hold the telescope still enough to see anything.

Sky watching

When you go outside, take a flashlight, so that you can read your star maps. To prevent the flashlight's glare stopping you from seeing well in the dark, cover the end with clear, red plastic film.

Don't give up if you can't see very much at first. Your eyes will adjust better to the darkness after about twenty minutes, and you will be able to see more stars.

STAR PHOTOGRAPHS

You don't have to be an expert in astronomy or photography to take some really good photos of the night sky. All you need is the right type of camera and film, and some ideas of what you would like to photograph.

An amateur photograph of comet Hale-Bopp, which could be seen in 1997.

What to look for

To find out what to look for at a particular time of year, look in astronomy magazines. They will tell you which of the constellations are in view and whether you can see any special events, such as a comet or meteor shower.

They will give you lots of star gazing tips and will also tell you about new and second-hand astronomy equipment. Newspapers will tell you about special events, too.

The constellation of Orion. You can clearly see Orion's Belt – the three middle stars.

Equipment

★ Camera. It must be an SLR (single lens reflex) type which has a shutter that can be held open. You can buy these second-hand. Ask for advice about inexpensive SLR cameras at a camera shop.

★ Something to place your camera on. A tripod is best, but if you don't want the expense of buying one you could just prop the camera on a low wall or car roof, resting it on a pillow or bean bag.

★ A shutter release cable to attach to your camera. This allows you to take a picture without touching – and possibly moving – the camera itself. They are not expensive.

★ A piece of dark cardboard, big enough to cover the camera lens. The shutter movement makes the camera shake slightly, and can result in blurred photographs. You can use the cardboard as described opposite to prevent this from happening.

★ Film. Ask a film supplier for a film that will record objects quickly where there is little light. A film with a rating of ISO 400, or higher, should do the trick.

★ A watch that shows seconds.

An SLR camera

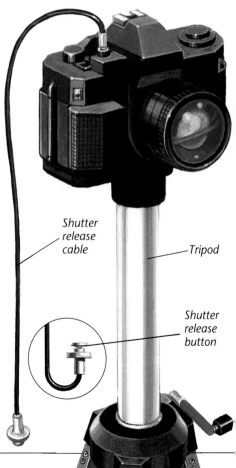

Shutter release cable

Tripod

Shutter release button

Taking photos

Your star photos will be much better if you take them from a dark place away from dazzling street lights. Here's what to do.

1. Place the camera on something stable, such as a tripod or a low wall, and aim it toward the sky at the object you want to photograph. Turn the focus ring until it is focused on infinity. Open the lens aperture to its widest – shown by the smallest F number.

2. After setting up the camera, leave it for about half an hour to get used to the temperature and conditions outside. Any condensation that may form on the lens will have time to disappear.

3. Place the cardboard in front of the lens. Press the button on the shutter release cable and hold it down. Wait for two seconds. Then take the cardboard away but keep holding down the shutter release button.

4. Count up to 20 seconds. Then put the cardboard back over the lens. Now let go of the shutter release button and listen for the "click". Then remove the cardboard from in front of the lens, wind on the film – and you're ready to take another picture.

Turn the focus ring until it is focused on infinity.

Open the aperture to its widest – shown by the smallest F number.

Star trails

Because the Earth spins, the stars appear to move across the sky during the night. To show this in a photo, follow the instructions on the left, but hold the shutter open for at least ten minutes.

The longer you hold open the shutter, the longer your star trails will be.

A picture like this can look stunning if you include a foreground object, such as a building, a tree, a distant hill or just the horizon.

An amateur photograph of star trails made by the Big Dipper (see page 63).

(see page 63)

Top tips

When you get your film processed, tell the assistant that the photos are of stars and to print all the frames. Otherwise, it might be assumed that the unusual results are mistakes and they may not be printed.

Try experimenting with different exposure times to see what gives you the best results.

Out and about

When you go outside to watch the stars or to take photos, make sure that you are warm and comfortable.

Even in warm weather, it can become chilly on a clear evening. Wear several layers of clothes and take a hat. If you are going out for more than an hour, take a snack and a hot drink.

Never go out in the dark alone. Go with a parent or guardian, or members of your astronomy club.

Saturn and Jupiter in the night sky taken by an amateur photographer.

TELESCOPES

There are two main types of telescopes for looking at the stars: reflector and refractor telescopes.

Reflector telescope

A reflector telescope uses a mirror to collect the light. It is usually less expensive than a refractor of the same power, but it needs more care. From time to time the mirror has to be re-aligned, and recoated with aluminum to make it reflect properly.

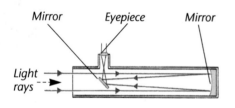

This diagram shows the path of light rays in a reflector telescope.

Refractor telescope

A refractor telescope uses a glass lens to collect the light. There is a labeled picture of a refractor telescope on page 77.

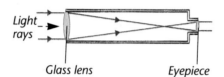

This diagram shows the path of light rays in a refractor telescope.

Telescope sizes

A telescope's power is measured by the size of the mirror or lens it uses. The larger the mirror or lens, the more light can be collected by the telescope and the clearer the image will be. It is not really worth buying a reflector telescope smaller than 100mm (4in) or a refractor telescope smaller than 75mm (3in).

Mountings

You will need a stand or mount to hold your telescope still. Many telescopes are sold complete with one. There are two kinds of mounts – altazimuth and equatorial.

An altazimuth mount allows you to move the telescope up and down (called altitude) and from side to side (called azimuth). It is easier to use than an equatorial mount.

An equatorial mount is set up to allow you to follow the curved path of a star across the sky with one movement.

Accessories

You can buy different parts to attach to your telescope.

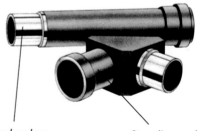

Barlow lens   Star diagonal

★ Barlow lens. This makes the magnification power of any eyepiece two or three times greater.

★ Star diagonal. This is a right-angle shaped mirror. Use it to look at high-up stars without bending down low.

A reflector telescope

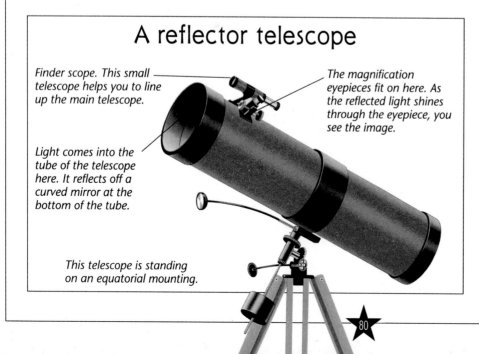

Finder scope. This small telescope helps you to line up the main telescope.

Light comes into the tube of the telescope here. It reflects off a curved mirror at the bottom of the tube.

The magnification eyepieces fit on here. As the reflected light shines through the eyepiece, you see the image.

This telescope is standing on an equatorial mounting.

ASTRONOMY FACTS AND LISTS

An Apollo astronaut exploring the Moon.

Here are some famous constellations with drawings of the things that they are supposed to represent. Compare the shape of the constellation to the drawing. You'll see that often the star pattern does not look much like the shape it represents.

Orion

The star scene shown on the right is dominated by Orion, a great hunter in Greek mythology. Armed with a club and a shield of lion skin, he faces a charging bull, Taurus. The easiest part of Orion to spot is the line of three stars which forms his belt. Below it lie two stars which represent his sword. Orion's two faithful hunting dogs, Canis Major and Canis Minor, stand behind him. At his feet is Lepus the hare, the animal he most enjoys hunting.

Aldebaran

Procyon

Betelgeuse

TAURUS

ORION

CANIS MINOR

Rigel

Sirius

LEPUS

The shape of Canis Major, the large dog, is quite easy to make out. However, you need more imagination to see the shape of the little dog, Canis Minor.

CANIS MAJOR

PEGASUS

Enif

ANDROMEDA

Algol

The story of Perseus

To ancient Greek astronomers, the stars on the left represented the myth of Perseus. He killed Medusa, a creature so ugly that anyone who looked at her turned to stone. On his way home, he found Andromeda, daughter of Cassiopeia and Cepheus. She was chained to the rocks, waiting to be devoured by the dreaded sea monster Cetus. Perseus showed Medusa's head to Cetus, who immediately turned to stone, and so Andromeda was saved from death.

Perseus cleverly used a mirrored shield to help him kill Medusa without looking straight at her. As Perseus cut off Medusa's head, the white, winged horse, Pegasus sprang from her neck.

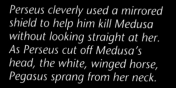

CASSIOPEIA

PERSEUS

MAP OF THE MOON

The map below shows the side of the Moon that always faces the Earth. This is the view you would see with the naked eye or using binoculars at full moon.

Most astronomical telescopes make things look upside down. If you are using a telescope, turn this book upside down, so that the picture will look like what you see.

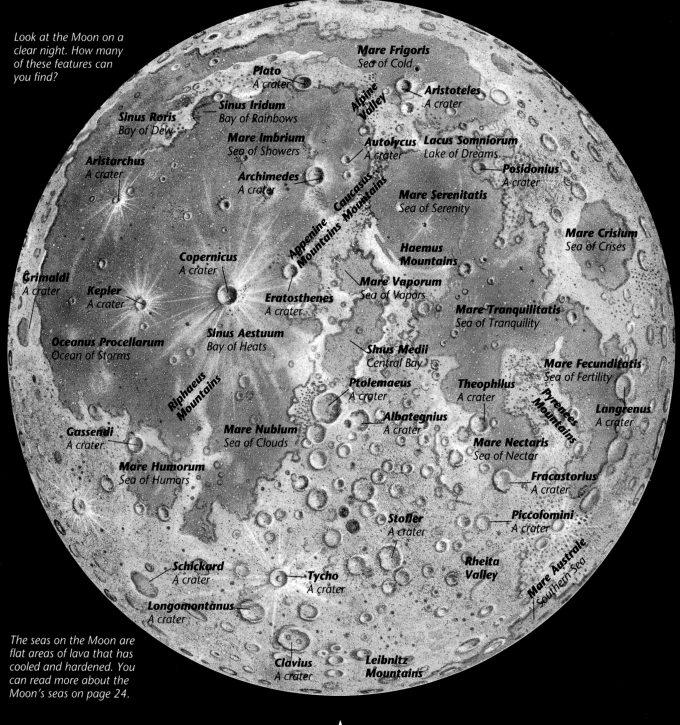

Look at the Moon on a clear night. How many of these features can you find?

Mare Frigoris
Sea of Cold

Plato
A crater

Aristoteles
A crater

Alpine Valley

Sinus Iridum
Bay of Rainbows

Sinus Roris
Bay of Dew

Mare Imbrium
Sea of Showers

Autolycus
A crater

Lacus Somniorum
Lake of Dreams

Posidonius
A crater

Aristarchus
A crater

Archimedes
A crater

Caucasus Mountains

Mare Serenitatis
Sea of Serenity

Mare Crisium
Sea of Crises

Appenine Mountains

Haemus Mountains

Copernicus
A crater

Grimaldi
A crater

Kepler
A crater

Eratosthenes
A crater

Mare Vaporum
Sea of Vapors

Mare Tranquilitatis
Sea of Tranquility

Oceanus Procellarum
Ocean of Storms

Sinus Aestuum
Bay of Heats

Sinus Medii
Central Bay

Mare Fecunditatis
Sea of Fertility

Ripheaus Mountains

Ptolemaeus
A crater

Theophilus
A crater

Pyrenees Mountains

Langrenus
A crater

Gassendi
A crater

Mare Nubium
Sea of Clouds

Albategnius
A crater

Mare Nectaris
Sea of Nectar

Mare Humorum
Sea of Humors

Fracastorius
A crater

Stofler
A crater

Piccolomini
A crater

Schickard
A crater

Rheita Valley

Mare Australe
Southern Sea

Tycho
A crater

Longomontanus
A crater

The seas on the Moon are flat areas of lava that has cooled and hardened. You can read more about the Moon's seas on page 24.

Clavius
A crater

Leibnitz Mountains

STARS AT-A-GLANCE

Satellites and space probes are always finding out new things about space. This means that what we know about the universe is always changing.

The lists on pages 84 to 86 show information about the different stars, nebulae, galaxies and meteor showers that are the most famous and easy to see.

Brightest stars

The stars are listed in order of their apparent magnitude, that is, how bright they look when viewed from the Earth.

Name of star	Name of constellation	Brightness (mag.)	Distance from Earth (light years)	Spectral type
Sirius	Canis Major	−1.46	8.6	A
Canopus	Carina	−0.72	1,200	F
Alpha Centauri	Centaurus	−0.27	4.3	G
Arcturus	Boötes	−0.04	37	K
Vega	Lyra	0.03	25.3	A
Capella	Auriga	0.08	42	G
Rigel	Orion	0.1 (variable)	910	B
Procyon	Canis Minor	0.38	11.3	F
Achernar	Eridanus	0.5	85	B
Betelgeuse	Orion	0.5 (variable)	310	M
Beta Centauri	Centaurus	0.6 (variable)	460	B
Altair	Aquila	0.77	16.8	A

Nearest stars to Earth

Name of star	Name of constellation	Brightness (mag.)	Distance from Earth (light years)	Spectral type
Proxima Centauri	Centaurus	11.1 (variable)	4.25	M
Alpha Centauri A	Centaurus	0	4.3	G
Beta Centauri B	Centaurus	1.4	4.3	K
Barnard's star	Ophiuchus	9.5	6	M
Wolf 359	Leo	13.5 (variable)	7.6	M
Lalande 21185	Ursa Major	7.5	8.1	M
UV Ceti A	Cetus	12.4 (variable)	8.4	M
UV Ceti B	Cetus	13.02 (variable)	8.4	M
Sirius A	Canis Major	−1.46	8.6	A
Sirius B	Canis Major	8.5	8.6	DA
Ross 154	Sagittarius	10.6	9.4	M
Ross 248	Andromeda	12.3	10.3	M

Double stars

Name of star	Name of constellation	Brightness (mag.)	Distance from Earth (light years)	Type of star
Alpha Capricorni	Capricornus	4.2, 3.6	1,600, 120	multiple star
Beta Capricorni	Capricornus	3.1, 6	250	physical double
Beta Cygni (Albireo)	Cygnus	3.1, 5.1	390	physical double
Nu Draconis	Draco	4.9, 4.9	120	physical double
Alpha Librae	Libra	2.8, 5.2	72	physical double
Epsilon Lyrae	Lyra	4.7, 5.1	120	double double
Zeta Lyrae	Lyra	4.4, 5.7	210	physical double
Theta Orionis (4 stars)	Orion	5.1, 6.7, 6.7, 8	1,300	multiple star
Theta Tauri	Taurus	3.4, 3.9	150	physical double
Zeta Ursae Majoris (Mizar and Alcor)	Ursa Major	2.3, 4	60, 80	optical double

Variable stars

Name of star	Name of constellation	Brightness (mag.)	Distance from Earth (light years)	Length of cycle	Type of star
Epsilon Aurigae	Auriga	3.3-4.1	4,564	27 years	eclipsing binary
Alpha Cassiopeia	Cassiopeia	2.2-3.1	120	irregular	irregular
Gamma Cassiopeia	Cassiopeia	1.6-3	780	irregular	shell star*
Delta Cephei	Cepheus	3.6-4.3	1,336	5 days 9 hours	pulsating variable
Mira	Cetus	2-10	94	331 days	long-period variable
Eta Geminorum	Gemini	3.1-4	190	233 days	double variable
Alpha Herculis	Hercules	3.1-3.9	218	semi-regular	double star
Beta Lyrae	Lyra	3.4-4.3	299	12 days 22 hours	eclipsing binary
Beta Persei	Perseus	2.2-3.5	95	2 days 21 hours	eclipsing binary
Betelgeuse	Orion	0.4-1.3	310	5 years 285 days	semi-regular

* A shell star rotates at such a high speed that it is unstable and throws off rings of gas. This causes the magnitude to vary.

Star clusters

Catalog number	Name of constellation	Brightness (mag.)	Distance from Earth (light years)	Type of cluster
M44 / NGC2632 (Praesepe)	Cancer	4	525	open
M41 / NGC2287	Canis Major	5	2,350	open
NGC5139 (Omega)	Centaurus	4	17,000	globular
NGC4755 (Jewel Box)	Crux	5	7,700	open
M35 / NGC2168	Gemini	5	2,200	open
M13 / NGC6205	Hercules	6	21,000-25,000	globular
M45 (Pleiades)	Taurus	1.5	410	open
NGC869/884 (double cluster)	Perseus	4	7,000/8,150	open
M47 / NGC2422	Puppis	6	1,540	open
NGC104 (47Tuc)	Tucana	4	15,000-20,000	globular
M22 / NGC6656	Sagittarius	5	9,600	globular
M7 / NGC6475	Scorpius	3	800	open

SPACE OBJECTS AT-A-GLANCE

Nebulae

Catalog number	Name of constellation	Name of nebula	Distance from Earth (light years)	Type of nebula
NGC7293	Aquarius	Helix	160-450	planetary
none	Crux	Coalsack	500-600	dark
NGC2070	Dorado	Tarantula	170,000	bright
M42	Orion	Great Nebula	1,300-1,900	bright
M8	Sagittarius	Lagoon	5,000	bright
M20	Sagittarius	Trifid	more than 5,000	bright
M17	Sagittarius	Omega	5,700	bright

Galaxies

Catalog number	Name of constellation	Name of galaxy	Distance from Earth (light years)	Type of galaxy
none	Dorado	Large Magellanic Cloud	170,000	irregular
NGC292	Tucana	Small Magellanic Cloud	205,000	irregular
M31	Andromeda	Great Spiral Galaxy	2,900,000	spiral
M33	Triangulum	Pinwheel	2,400,000	spiral
M51	Canes Venatici	Whirlpool Galaxy	35,000,000	spiral
M81	Ursa Major	none	7,000,000-9,000,000	spiral
M82	Ursa Major	none	7,000,000-9,000,000	irregular

Major annual meteor showers

A meteor shower is a short but spectacular display of meteors caused by the Earth moving across the orbit of a comet.

Dates visible	Peak time	Name of meteor shower	Associated comet	Name of constellation	No. per hour at peak time
Jan 1-6	4 Jan	Quadrantids	-	Boötes	60
Apr 19-25	21 April	Lyrids	Thatcher	Lyra	10
Apr 24-May 20	5 May	Eta Aquarids	Halley	Aquarius	35
Jul 25-Aug 20	12 Aug	Perseids	Swift-Tuttle	Perseus	75
Oct 16-21	22 Oct	Orionids	Halley	Orion	25
Oct 20-Nov 30	3 Nov	Taurids	Encke	Taurus	10
Nov 15-19	17 Nov	Leonids	Tempel-Tuttle	Leo	variable
Dec 7-15	13 Dec	Geminids	Phaeton (asteroid)	Gemini	75

Astronomical symbols

Astronomers use special symbols to represent the Sun, Moon, planets and the twelve constellations of the Zodiac.

Sun	Moon	Mercury	Venus	Earth	Mars	Jupiter	Saturn	Uranus	Neptune	Pluto

Aquarius	Pisces	Aries	Taurus	Gemini	Cancer	Leo	Virgo	Libra	Scorpius	Sagittarius	Capricornus

The planets at-a-glance

Name of planet	Diameter of planet	Average distance from Sun	Time to orbit Sun	Time to rotate	Number of satellites
Mercury	4,880km (3,032 miles)	58 million km (36 million miles)	88 days	59 days	None
Venus	12,100km (7,518 miles)	108 million km (67 million miles)	225 days	243 days	None
Earth	12,756km (7,926 miles)	150 million km (93 million miles)	365.3 days	23hrs 56mins	1 (Moon)
Mars	6,786km (4,217 miles)	228 million km (142 million miles)	687 days	24hrs 37mins	2
Jupiter	142,984km (88,846 miles)	778 million km (483 million miles)	11.9 years	9hrs 50mins	16
Saturn	120,536km (74,898 miles)	1,427 million km (887 million miles)	29.5 years	10hrs 14mins	18
Uranus	51,118km (31,763 miles)	2,871 million km (1,784 million miles)	84 years	17hrs 54mins	15
Neptune	49,528km (30,775 miles)	4,500 million km (2,796 million miles)	165 years	19hrs 12mins	8
Pluto	2,400km (1,491 miles)	5,913 million km (3,674 million miles)	248 years	6 days 10hrs	1

Planetary satellites

Planet	Name of satellite (year discovered)			
Earth	Moon (-)			
Mars	Deimos (1877)	Phobos (1877)		
Jupiter	Adrastea (1979)	Almathea (1892)	Ananke (1951)	Callisto (1610)
	Carme (1938)	Elara (1905)	Europa (1610)	Ganymede (1610)
	Himalia (1904)	Io (1610)	Leda (1974)	Lysithea (1938)
	Metis (1989)	Pasiphae (1908)	Sinope (1914)	Thebe (1979)
Saturn	Atlas (1980)	Calypso (1980)	Dione (1684)	Dione B (1982)
	Enceladus (1789)	Epimetheus (1980)	Hyperion (1848)	Iapetus (1671)
	Janus (1980)	Mimas (1789)	1980 S26 (1980)	1980 S27 (1980)
	1990 S18 (1990)	Phoebe (1898)	Rhea (1672)	Telesto (1980)
	Tethys (1684)	Titan (1655)		
Uranus	Ariel (1851)	Belinda (1986)	Bianca (1986)	Cordelia (1986)
	Cressida (1986)	Desdemona (1986)	Juliet (1986)	Miranda (1948)
	Oberon (1787)	Ophelia (1986)	Portia (1986)	Puck (1986)
	Rosalind (1986)	Titania (1787)	Umbriel (1851)	
Neptune	Nereid (1949)	1989 N1 (1989)	1989 N2 (1989)	1989 N3 (1989)
	1989 N4 (1989)	1989 N5 (1989)	1989 N6 (1989)	Triton (1846)
Pluto	Charon (1978)			

Where to look

Mercury, Venus, Mars, Jupiter, Saturn and Uranus can all be seen with the naked eye. But they do not always appear in the same place in the sky.

Astronomy magazines and some newspapers print details of what is visible in the night sky and where to look.

LANDMARKS OF ASTRONOMY

These two pages give you a quick history of astronomy. They tell you when people made important discoveries that contributed to our knowledge of outer space.

3100BC* The Egyptians begin using calendars to figure out when they should plant and harvest their crops. The calendars are calculated according to the positions of the stars.

3000BC The oldest known constellation shapes are drawn around this time, by the Egyptians.

2446BC Chinese astronomers notice that five planets (Mercury, Venus, Earth, Mars and Jupiter) have moved into line with one another. This shows that people have become aware that the planets move in space.

6000BC-AD**100 Astronomy is studied in great detail in Greece and becomes one of the sciences taught in Greek universities.

300BC-AD900 In Central America, the Mayas are interested in astronomy. Using their findings, they devise an accurate calendar – later adopted by the Aztecs.

AD150 Greek astronomer Ptolemy publishes his Ptolemeic System. According to this, the Earth is in the middle of the universe. Everything else, including the Sun, orbits the Earth. Astronomers follow this idea for the next 1,400 years.

Ptolemy

*The years before the birth of Jesus Christ have BC ("before Christ") written after them. The bigger the number, the longer ago it happened.
**The years after the birth of Jesus Christ sometimes have AD before them. (AD stands for the Latin "anno Domini" meaning "in the year of our Lord".)

200-1000 The study of astronomy stops in Europe during this time. Due to frequent wars and lack of food, people's struggle to survive means that science and learning suffer. Modern astronomers call these years the lost centuries.

1006 The Lupus Supernova is observed by the Chinese. Shining almost as brightly as a quarter Moon for nearly two months, it is the brightest supernova ever. For a time, it is even visible in broad daylight.

Around 1000 The astronomy revival begins in Arabia. The subject is taught once more at Baghdad University.

1030 Astronomer Al-Sufi, from the Baghdad School of Astronomy, draws up the best of the many star catalogs that begin to appear at this time.

1054 The Taurus Supernova is noted by the Chinese. The debris from this supernova can still be seen as the Crab Nebula.

1420 Samarkand Observatory is built in Central Asia by Ulegh Beg.

1543 Copernicus publishes *De Revolutionibus Orbium Coelestium* ("On the Revolution of the Heavenly Spheres"), a controversial book which suggests that the Sun is at the middle of the Solar System.

1572 Denmark. Tycho Brahe observes a supernova.

1604 "Kepler's Nova" is seen in our galaxy by the German astronomer, Johannes Kepler.

1608 A simple refractor telescope is invented by Hans Lippershey in the Netherlands.

1609 Italian astronomer Galileo Galilei builds a telescope which is

an improvement on Lippershey's telescope. With it, Galileo begins his observations of the stars and planets.

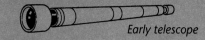
Early telescope

1668 England. Isaac Newton builds the first reflector telescope.

1687 England. Newton publishes a book, *Principia*. In it, he proves that the Earth and other planets orbit the Sun.

1758 A comet returns as predicted by the English scientist Edmund Halley in 1705. It is named Halley's Comet in his memory.

1781 France. Comet-hunter Charles Messier publishes a catalog of nebulae, galaxies and star clusters.

1781 England. William Herschel discovers Uranus.

1801 Italy. The first asteroid is discovered by Giuseppe Piazzi.

1845 Ireland. The Earl of Rosse builds the biggest, most powerful reflector telescope yet made. Called Leviathan, it has a 1.93m (76in) mirror. Using Leviathan, astronomers discover spiral galaxies.

1846 France. Neptune is discovered by Johann Gottfried Galle and Heinrich Louis D'Arrest.

1877 England. Mars's two moons, Phobos and Deimos, are discovered by Asaph Hall.

Italy. Giovanni Schiaparelli observes deep channels, the "canals", on Mars.

1910 Halley's Comet is seen again. The Great Daylight Comet is also seen. It is so bright that it can be spotted during the day.

1915-17 Following on from his Special Theory of Relativity, the German scientist Albert Einstein develops his General Theory of Relativity. This theory revolutionizes the way scientists research space, gravity, time and physics.

1927 Belgium. Georges Lemaître proposes that the universe was formed in a huge explosion – the Big Bang theory.

1930 U.S.A. Pluto is discovered by Clyde Tombaugh.

1937 U.S.A. Groter Reber invents the first true radio telescope.

1946 U.S.A. Edwin Hubble helps to build Hale, the biggest reflector telescope yet made. It has a 5.08m (200in) mirror.

1948 England. The Big Bang theory is challenged by the Steady State theory of scientists Hermann Bondi and Thomas Gold. This theory says that the universe will always look the same.

1957 Soviet Union. Sputnik 1, the world's first artificial satellite, is launched on October 4. On November 3, Sputnik 2 is launched, carrying a dog, called Laika, into space.

1959 The first space probes are sent to the Moon by the Soviet Union.

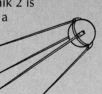

Sputnik 1

1961 Soviet Union. On April 12, Yuri Gagarin becomes the first person to go into space. The flight lasts less than two hours.

1963 Soviet Union. On June 16, Valentina Tereshkova becomes the first woman to go into space. The flight lasts for nearly three days.

1965 U.S.A. Arno Penzias and Robert Wilson detect weak signals, like radio noise, from space. Many people think that this proves that the Big Bang really happened.

1965 U.S. space probe Mariner 4 takes the first photographs of Mars.

1966 Soviet space probe Luna 9 is the first to land on the Moon.

1967 The Soviet Union lands the first space probe on Venus.

1968 The U.S.A. makes the first manned space flight, Apollo 8, around the Moon.

1969 On July 20, the U.S. Apollo 11 mission lands the first men on the Moon. They are Neil Armstrong and Buzz Aldrin. Neil Armstrong becomes the first man to walk on the Moon.

U.S.A. First sighting of a pulsar (seen in the Crab Nebula) is made by astronomers at Steward Observatory.

1971 U.S. Mariner 9 space probe returns the first ever close-up pictures of Mars.

1973 The U.S.A. launches Skylab, the first space station.

U.S. Pioneer 10 spacecraft returns the first ever close-up pictures of Jupiter.

1974 U.S. Mariner 10 space probe returns the first photos of Venus's cloud tops and Mercury's surface.

1975 Soviet space probes Venera 9 and Venera 10 return the first photos of Venus's surface.

1976 U.S. space probes Viking 1 and Viking 2 land on Mars. They take extensive pictures and samples of the planet's soil.

1977 The Chiron asteroid is discovered by Charles Kowal, an American astronomer. The rings around Uranus are discovered.

1979 The existence of Pluto's Moon Charon is confirmed.

U.S. space probes, Voyager 1 and Voyager 2, fly past Jupiter, sending back detailed pictures.

1980 U.S. space probe Voyager 2 flies past Saturn. It sends back detailed pictures.

1981 On April 12, the U.S.A. launches STS1, the first space shuttle flight.

1986 U.S. probe Voyager 2 flies past Uranus. It sends detailed images.

Soviet space station Mir is launched.

U.S. space shuttle Challenger explodes, killing seven astronauts.

1987 A supernova is observed in the Large Magellanic Cloud. It is the brightest supernova sighted for several hundred years.

1989 U.S. space probe Voyager 2 flies past Neptune. It sends back detailed pictures.

1990 The Hubble Space Telescope is launched from the U.S.A. It is found to have a fault, preventing it from sending detailed images of distant parts of space.

1991 The Hubble Space Telescope is repaired by spacewalking astronauts.

1991 U.S. Galileo space probe takes close-up pictures of the asteroid Gaspra. They are the first close-up pictures of an asteroid.

1995 Comet Hale-Bopp is discovered. Astronomers predict that it will be at its brightest in 1997.

The Hubble Space Telescope being repaired

1997 Comet Hale-Bopp becomes the brightest comet since 1911.

U.S. Mars Pathfinder reaches Mars. It sends back detailed information about the planet's soil, rocks and weather.

In October the U.S.A. launches the Cassini mission to Saturn.

QUESTIONS AND ANSWERS

Q
Many scientists think that the universe started with a massive explosion, called the Big Bang. What was there before this?

A
According to scientists, there was nothing before the Big Bang. Time itself started with the Big Bang.

Q
Is it true that you can see the past by looking out into space?

A
Yes. When you look out deep into space, you are actually seeing light that set out from distant points many, many years ago. The farther away something is, the longer the light has taken to reach you and so the further back in time you are looking when you see it. For example, we see the Sun as it was eight minutes ago, Alpha Centauri as it was four years ago, and the Andromeda Galaxy as it was 2.9 million years ago. Scientists believe that the most distant objects are so far back in time that they give clues about the beginning of the universe.

Q
How big is a black hole?

A
Nobody is sure, because nobody has actually seen a black hole! Scientists believe that the distance across black holes may range from the distance across a small town to the distance across a giant planet, such as Jupiter, or even bigger.

Q
Can you see other galaxies from Earth?

A
Yes. Using powerful telescopes, many thousands of galaxies can be seen. Even with the naked eye, you can see three: the Large Magellanic Cloud, the Small Magellanic Cloud, and M31, the Andromeda Galaxy. (See pages 67 and 71).

Q
How much longer will the Sun last?

A
Scientists believe that the Sun should last for about another 4,500 million to 5,000 million years.

Q
How many stars are there in space?

A
Nobody knows for sure. There are about 100,000 million stars in the Milky Way galaxy alone. Astronomers now believe that there are many millions of galaxies in the universe, each with as many stars as our own Milky Way. We will probably never know just how many stars there are.

Q
Why do stars twinkle?

A
As a star's light passes through the Earth's atmosphere, it is bent and broken up. The angle that it bends depends on the temperature of the air. The light passes through both warm and cold air, so it shines at us from different directions at once. The star then appears to flicker.

Star light bending on its way through the Earth's atmosphere.

Q
If you want to find out where north is, Polaris, the northern pole star, points the way. Thuban used to be the northern pole star. How and why has it changed?

A
The Earth spins at an angle but it wobbles as it spins. This means that over thousands of years, the angle at which it spins changes. The wobble causes the north pole gradually to point in a different direction, eventually pointing at a different star.

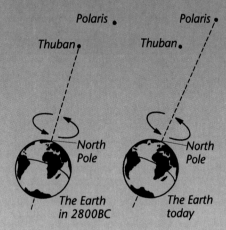

Q
Could spacecraft land on all the planets in the Solar System?

A
No, only on the solid planets: Mercury, Venus, Earth, Mars and Pluto. Jupiter, Saturn, Uranus and Neptune are all "gas giants", huge balls of gas and liquid with no solid surface. There are, however, plenty of moons which a spacecraft could land on instead.

Q
What does the night sky look like on the Moon?

A
The Moon has no atmosphere so the sky there is always clear. When the Sun is in the sky, it is so bright that it blocks out all the stars, but when it sets, you can see the stars much more clearly than you can from Earth. You can see the Earth in the sky too, looking like a large blue and white marble. With binoculars you can see countries and even some cities. Like the Moon, the Earth goes through phases.

Q

Why is Mars red?

A

Mars's soil contains lots of iron, which has rusted away over millions of years. Rusty iron is red.

Q

Some people claim to have seen aliens. Do they really exist?

A

Nobody knows whether or not aliens exist. Lots of people claim to have seen them but there is no proof. Scientists now think that there are lots of other stars in our own galaxy with their own planets, and so with millions of galaxies in the universe, there could be countless billions of planets out there. Experts now think that there are several places in our own Solar System where there are chemicals which could enable life to exist. These chemicals have been found on Mars, and beneath the icy surface of Europa, one of Jupiter's moons. So far, however, nobody has found alien life in any of them.

Q

How many asteroids are there in the Solar System?

A

Nobody is sure of the exact number of asteroids in the Solar System, but there are certainly thousands. There are so many of them, not only in the Asteroid Belt, but dotted around space, that it is doubtful that they will ever be counted.

Q

Has anyone on Earth ever been hit by a meteorite?

A

Yes, but don't worry too much as it doesn't happen very often. In the early 1990s, for example, a man was struck by a meteorite while driving his car on a highway in Germany. An unlucky dog was killed by a falling meteorite in the early 1900s.

Q

What is the biggest comet ever seen?

A

The Great Comet of 1811 had a coma that was over 2 million km (1¼ million miles) wide – wider than the Sun. The Great Comet of 1843 had a tail that was 330 million km (about 200 million miles) long – that's long enough to stretch from the Sun to Mars.

Q

Can you see satellites from Earth?

A

Yes, they look like stars which move slowly across the sky. Some appear to blink very slowly, unlike planes which flash relatively quickly. You can see a satellite somewhere in the sky every few minutes.

Q

How do you become an astronaut?

A

The best way to become an astronaut is first to become a scientist, for example a chemist, astronomer or engineer. You will need a university degree and a specialization in a branch of science which is relevant to outer space. It is also useful to learn to fly a plane. Then apply to NASA and ask if they will accept you as an Astronaut Candidate. If they take you on, you may need to train for four or five years. Eventually, you may be lucky enough to be selected for a mission.

Q

Do you have to be a scientist to go into space?

A

No, although most people who go into space are scientists. They conduct useful investigations, for example into the effects of life in space on the human body. It is becoming more common for non-scientists to take part in space missions, and it is predicted that in the early part of the twenty-first century, space tourism will begin. This means that, in theory, anybody who is fit enough to travel in space will be able to take a short trip into orbit. However, space trips will be very, very expensive, so you'll have to be rich as well as fit.

Q

Why do space missions always have to blast off? Why can't they just take off, like planes do?

A

Jet engines need lots of air in order to work. They cannot work in the thin air at the edges of the Earth's atmosphere, so they can't be used to power spacecraft. At present, the only alternative is rockets. They blast energy out of their exhaust jets at an incredible rate, and push the spacecraft upward at a tremendous speed. Scientists are currently working on ways to make jet engines which will work at the edge of the atmosphere. At the moment, space shuttles are the only craft that can land like a plane, but they still need to blast off with a rocket.

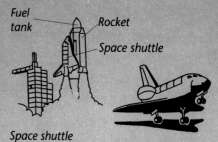

Fuel tank

Rocket

Space shuttle

Space shuttle blastoff

Space shuttle landing

Q

How long would it take for a group of astronauts to travel to Pluto?

A

If astronauts flew in an Apollo spacecraft (the type that flew to the Moon), it would take them about 86 years to reach Pluto.

Q

In some science fiction movies, people are transported instantly by being de-materialized and then beamed to another place. Is this really possible?

A

No. To transport a person instantly from one place to another, all of the atoms that make up a person's body would have to be pulled apart, whizzed through space and then rebuilt in exactly the same pattern. As atoms are always moving, it would be nearly impossible to put them back together in the right order.

GLOSSARY

This glossary explains the meaning of important words to do with astronomy and space. Words in bold type are explained elsewhere in the glossary.

asterism Small, easily-recognized pattern of **stars**, usually forming part of a larger pattern, or **constellation**.

asteroid Small, rocky object orbiting the **Sun**. Thousands of them exist in the part of the **Solar System** known as the Asteroid Belt, between Mars and Jupiter.

astronomy The scientific study of the universe and the objects in it.

atmosphere A layer of gas that surrounds a **planet** or **star**.

aurora A display of light in the upper **atmosphere** near a **planet's** poles. Caused by **solar wind**.

Big Bang theory A theory which states that the **universe** began in an enormous explosion.

binary star Two **stars** that revolve around one another, locked together by each other's **gravity**.

black hole An invisible region in space that has an enormous pull of **gravity**. Caused by a collapsed **supergiant star**.

cataclysmic variable A type of **binary star** system where, from time to time, one star gains some of the other star's **matter**. As this happens, a huge amount of light is given off.

cluster A group of **stars** or **galaxies** that lie close together.

coma The huge cloud of gas around the icy **nucleus** of a **comet**.

comet A chunk of dirty, dark ice, mixed with dust and grit which revolves around the **Sun** in an oval **orbit**.

constellation A group of **stars** that can be seen as a pattern from Earth. There are 88 constellations.

core The central part of a **planet**, **moon** or **asteroid**. It is made of different materials from its surrounding layers.

corona The outermost part of the **Sun's atmosphere**.

crater A hollow in the surface of a **planet**, **moon** or **asteroid**, caused by the impact of a **meteorite** or an **asteroid**.

crust The outer part of a **planet** or **moon**, made mostly of rock.

day The length of time it takes a **planet** to spin around once.

dwarf star A **star** which is smaller than the **Sun**.

eclipse The total or partial blocking of one object in space by another. For example, when the **Moon** passes in front of the **Sun**, the Sun is eclipsed.

eclipsing variable A type of **binary star**, where one of the stars passes in front of the other, resulting in a dip in brightness.

equator The imaginary line around the middle of a **planet**, dividing its northern **hemisphere** from its southern hemisphere.

facula A cloud of glowing gases that surrounds a **sunspot**, hovering just above the **Sun's** surface.

galaxy A group of **stars**, **nebulae**, **star clusters**, **globular clusters** and other **matter**. There are millions of galaxies in the **universe**.

gas giant A type of planet which is made up of gas and liquids surrounding a relatively small **core**.

giant star A star which is larger than the **Sun**.

gravity The force of attraction that pulls a smaller object toward a more massive object. For example, the **Moon** is attracted to the Earth by gravity.

hemisphere Half of a **planet** or **moon**. The top half is the northern hemisphere and the bottom half is the southern hemisphere.

light year The distance that a ray of light travels in one year: 9.46 million million km (5.88 million million miles).

magnitude A **star's** brightness.

matter Tiny particles from which everything is made.

meteor A **meteoroid** that travels through the Earth's **atmosphere**. As it falls toward Earth, it burns up, making a streak of light. Also known as a **shooting star**.

meteorite A **meteor** that hits the Earth's surface.

meteoroid Dust or a small chunk of rock which **orbits** the **Sun**.

meteor shower A short but spectacular display of **meteors** caused by the Earth moving across the **orbit** of a **comet**.

Milky Way A broad band of light that looks like a trail of spilled milk in the night sky. Created by the millions of faint **stars** that form part of our **galaxy**.

Milky Way galaxy The **galaxy** that contains the **Solar System**.

moon Any natural object which **orbits** a **planet**.

Moon The ball of rock which **orbits** the Earth.

multiple system A **star** system containing two or more stars.

NASA The National Aeronautics and Space Administration, which organizes space exploration on behalf of the government of the U.S.A. Projects include the Space Shuttle missions.

nebula A vast cloud of gas and dust where new **stars** often form.

neutron star A small, spinning **star** that is left when a **supergiant star** has exploded.

nova A **star** that suddenly increases in brightness and then fades away. A type of **cataclysmic variable** star.

nuclear fusion A type of activity that goes on inside a **star**, where tiny particles (called atoms) of gas join together to make larger atoms. This process creates huge amounts of heat and light.

nucleus The central point around which other things are arranged. In astronomy, the word is used to refer to the dense part in the middle of a **galaxy** or at the head of a **comet**.

optical double star Two **stars** that appear very close together when seen from Earth, because they are in the same line of sight. However, they are not linked to one another in any way.

orbit The path of one object as it revolves around another. For example, the **planets** orbit the **Sun**.

penumbra An area of light shadow caused by the partial **eclipse** of one object by another.

phase A particular stage in a cycle of changes that occurs over and over again. For example, the **Moon's** appearance goes through several phases as it travels around the Earth every month.

physical double star Another name for a **binary star.**

planet A relatively large object that revolves around a **star**, but which is not itself a star. There are nine known **planets** in our **Solar System**.

planetary nebula Outer layers of gas from a dying **star**, which are puffed into space. From a distance, the layers of glowing gas around the dying star make it look like a **planet**.

planisphere A movable, circular map of the **stars** in the sky that can be made to show the appearance of the night sky at any given time and date.

pointers Two or more **stars** in a **constellation** that show the way to another constellation.

pole One of the two points on a **planet's** surface that are farthest away from its equator.

primary star The brighter **star** in an **eclipsing variable**.

prominence A cloud of gas that bursts out from the **Sun's** surface.

pulsar A **neutron star** that sends out beams of **radiation** which swing around as the star spins.

pulsating variable A **star** which changes in size, temperature and brightness.

radar A method of finding the position and speed of distant objects using beams of radio waves.

radiation The waves of energy, heat or particles from an object.

red giant Type of star that has a relatively low temperature and is many times larger than the **Sun**.

satellite Any object in outer space that **orbits** another object. Man-made satellites are launched into space to orbit a **planet** or **moon**.

secondary star The fainter **star** in an **eclipsing variable**.

shooting star Another name for a **meteor**.

solar Something that relates to the Sun, such as a **solar flare**, or **solar wind**.

solar flare A sudden outburst of energy from a small part of the Sun's surface.

Solar System The **Sun** and all the objects that **orbit** it.

solar wind A constant stream of invisible particles that is blown from the Sun's surface into space.

spacecraft A vehicle made to travel in space.

space probe An unmanned **spacecraft** which collects information about objects in space and sends it back to scientists on Earth.

space shuttle A **spacecraft** which carries people and materials into space. It is launched by a rocket but lands like a plane and can be used again.

space station A large, manned **satellite** in space used as a base for space exploration over a long period of time.

spectral type A class of **star**, shown by the letters O, B, A, F, G, K and M.

star A ball of constantly exploding gases, giving off light and heat. The Sun is a star.

Sun A medium-sized **star** that lies in the middle of our **Solar System**.

sunspot One of the dark patches that appear on the **Sun** every now and again.

supergiant stars The brightest **giant stars**. They live for only a few million years.

supernova The explosion of a **supergiant star** which generates enormous amounts of light. The star then collapses to form a **neutron star**, or if the star was very large, a **black hole**.

tail The stream of visible gases that comes off a **comet** as it passes relatively close to the **Sun**.

umbra An area of dark shadow caused by the **eclipse** of one object by another.

universe The word used to describe everything that exists in space, including the **galaxies** and **stars**, the **Milky Way** and the **Solar System**.

variable star A **star** whose brightness changes over time, usually in a predictable way.

white dwarf A type of **star** that is much smaller and denser than the **Sun**. It gives off a relatively dim, white light.

year The length of time it takes a **planet** to **orbit** the **Sun**.

INDEX

Constellations and asterisms are listed in bold type, stars are listed in italics.

Useful addresses

Australia
Sydney Observatory
Observatory Hill,
Watson Road,
The Rocks,
New South Wales

Canada
Royal Astronomical Society of Canada
136 Dupont Street
Toronto ON
M5R 1V2

Federation des Groupes d'Astronomes
    Amateurs
4545 Avenue Pierre-de-Coubertin
Casier Postal 1000
Succursale M
Montreal QC
H1V 3RZ

Great Britain
British Astronomical Association
Burlington House
Piccadilly
London W1V 9AG

Federation of Astronomical Societies
c/o Clive Down
10 Glanyllyn
Bridgend
County Borough
CF33 4EF
(Please enclose stamped addressed envelope)

New Zealand
Royal Astronomical Society of New Zealand
P.O. Box 3181
Wellington

Dunedin Astronomical Society
P.O. Box 6019
Dunedin

New Zealand Spaceflight Association, Inc.
P.O. Box 2945
Wellington

USA
Amateur Astronomers Association
1010 Park Avenue
New York NY
10028

Use the Internet

There is a huge amount of information about space on the Internet. To find it, enter a space word in your Internet provider's search engine. For example, to find information on stars, enter the word `stars`.

You could also search the Internet to find information about an astronomy club near you. Do your search by entering the phrase `astronomy clubs` in a search engine.

NASA's homepage is at `http://www.nasa.gov` with links to superb space images and up-to-date information from the world's biggest space exploring organization.

Look at the Space Telescope Science Institute's homepage at `http://www.stsci.edu` for information about the Hubble Space Telescope and images of its amazing findings.

Published by Scholastic Inc., 555 Broadway, New York, NY 10012, by arrangement with Usborne Publishing Ltd. SCHOLASTIC and associated logos are trademarks and/or registered trademarks of Scholastic Inc.

12 11 10 9 8 7 6 5 4 3   9/9 0 1 2 3/0

ISBN 439-07728-1

Printed in the U.S.A.

First Scholastic printing, October 1998

14